Starting
a Sudbury School

A Summary of the
Experiences of
Fifteen Start-up Groups

D1607589

Daniel Greenberg and Mimsy Sadofsky

Sudbury Valley School Press®
Framingham, Massachusetts

ISBN: 1-888947-19-5

Table of Contents

"Maybe potential founders could get a taste of what it is like before they actually commit themselves to it, by going into a commercial laundromat, getting inside one of those industrial dryers, putting it on an hour-long cycle—and having it get stuck and go for a week instead."

Foreword

For some time now people have been hoping to have available a simple guide summarizing the various steps that have to be taken in order to found a Sudbury school. The School Planning Kit, available from the Sudbury Valley School Press, contains a wealth of information about various facets of the model, including a publication that deals specifically with the details of getting a school going, *Announcing A New School*, which discusses the founding of Sudbury Valley, in 1967-1969. However, for some time now, the need has been felt for a more current work, a work which takes advantage of the experiences of diverse groups, as well as one that deals with more contemporary experiences.

In the Fall of 1995, with the support of Sudbury Valley School's Public Relations Committee, we embarked on a study of the experiences of various schools and groups for the express purpose of filling this need. We visited fourteen schools and groups throughout the country conducting extensive, taped interviews, and collecting materials from each. In addition, we called upon the information that had been gathered from these and other schools and groups during some eight years of working with people who were trying to start schools and keep them going.

This report is the distillation of our study. We have tried to keep it focussed enough to be useful as a guide without pretending to seek to produce a template. Anyone seeking to delve into our source materials more extensively is welcome to contact us to explore the feasibility of doing so.

This work contains dozens of quotes, based on the particular speaker's experience, that are pointed summaries of a particular subject under discussion. We have used these quotes without attribution in order to protect the privacy of our sources, to whom we had assured confidentiality. In general we have tried to mask the identity of the specific groups whose experiences we are referring to, and we have replaced the names of individuals with unrelated initials.

We would like to thank the dozens of people across the country who took the time and trouble to prepare themselves in advance, to make themselves available to us for long interviews, and to collect archival material for our use. In a very real sense, any beneficial results that emerge from this study are due directly to their efforts.

Daniel Greenberg
Mimsy Sadofsky
1997

What kind of folks get going

The primary founders who have put their energy into getting Sudbury schools going are striking in their diversity. They come from all walks of life: housewives, teachers, professors, business-people, therapists, artists, carpenters, health-care professionals, musicians, and computer specialists. They come in all ages, from the twenties up. There are more women than men, but most groups have both genders well-represented. Some are from the upper middle class, but most are from the lower and mid middle class. Some come from rural or small-town backgrounds, others are from big cities. Most have some post-high school education; some have master's degrees or doctorates. Many found their traditional schooling exceptionally traumatic and damaging; others enjoyed it tremendously, and did extremely well. The majority of founders are parents interested in starting a school for their children, but some groups start mainly through the efforts of non-parents. The family backgrounds of many are traditional and/or religious, of others, secular and/or liberal. Among the founders, many different religions are represented, and there are also people with no known religious beliefs. There are New Age types, followers of various esoteric teachings, and people with very traditional world views. Every political view from left to right is represented.

Here are a few sample configurations of the original founding groups of schools that survived their first two years.

One founder
    businessperson/parent

Two founders
    social activist/parent; artist/parent

Three founders
    teacher/parent; teacher/parent; teacher/parent
    teacher/parent; teacher; software consultant/parent
    nurse/social activist/retailer/parent/homeschooler;
        graphic artist/parent/homeschooler; teacher/
        parent/homeschooler

Four founders
    educator/parent; therapist/parent/homeschooler;
        therapist/parent/homeschooler; businessperson/
        parent

Five founders
    court transcriber/parent/homeschooler; pharmacist/
        parent; photographer/parent; traffic engineer/
        parent/homeschooler; child-care provider/
        parent/homeschooler
    restauranteur/therapist/parent; therapist/antique art
        dealer/parent; parent; carpenter/handyman/
        education student; member of intentional
        community/childbirth educator/parent

Here are a few sample configurations of the original
founding groups of schools that opened but did not survive
more than two years.

One founder
   real-estate analyst; contractor/parent

Two founders
   therapist/parent; therapist/acupuncturist/parent
   editor/parent; photographer/parent/homeschooler
   international businessman/parent; laborer/parent

Five founders
   nurse/parent/homeschooler; parent/homeschooler;
   "back to the land" advocate/parent; day care
   centeradministrator/parent/homeschooler; health
   care center administrator/parent

Clearly, there is no way of making generalizations about the type of person who is likely to become a founder of a Sudbury school.

The conclusion to be reached is that as one searches for others to work with in such an endeavor, one must be completely open-minded and free of pre-conceptions about who may or may not be attracted to the ideas. This work creates strange bedfellows.

There does however seem to be one characteristic that is typical of all primary founders of schools that ultimately manage to open and stay alive for some period of time: a "can-do" attitude—a determination to overcome every obstacle, to keep going no matter what, to work as hard as necessary regardless of the personal cost in time and energy.

What gets folks going

How does it happen that a founding group first gets going? There must be at least one person who has thought long and hard about wanting something very different in education. Founders often have come to some conclusions about what it is they want—perhaps from exposure to SVS literature; from having read *Summerhill*, John Holt, or other books about alternative education; from unhappy personal experiences with education, either as a student or as a teacher; or from general philosophical considerations about child development. They may have had childhood dreams about a better way to spend one's days than going to a traditional school, or have children who are uncomfortable in schools they attend now. Sometimes they are home-schoolers (or home-"unschoolers") who are looking for broader social and intellectual exposure for their children. Usually they are compassionate and sensitive people who wish to provide a more wholesome environment for children than that generally available today.

In fact, a great many people fit this general description of a founder, but only a very small number actually go on to start schools. Besides the motivation, there have to be catalytic events in their personal lives that push them towards thinking about starting a school themselves, and in particular (as it applies to our topic) about starting a Sudbury school. For example:

- Two people in a mid-Atlantic state, one with a young child, both studying to be certified as teachers, were visiting a number of schools. After one such visit, they suddenly realized that they couldn't function in any of the contexts to which they had been exposed. Some years later, having founded an alternative school, they and their colleagues came across the book *Free at Last* and immediately realized that it represented what they were really looking for.

• A woman in New England, homeschooling her two children, read an article in *Mothering* about Sudbury Valley. After further investigating the school, she attended an evening during which SVS alumni talked about their lives. She immediately became obsessed with creating such a place for her own children.

• A woman in the Pacific Northwest read the same article in *Mothering* and began a long series of exploratory meetings with people to whom she networked; a very similar set of events triggered the founding of a school in California.

• Other people in a neighboring Pacific Northwest community attended a talk about Sudbury Valley which galvanized them into action.

• A teacher in an alternative public school program in a Rocky Mountain state was exposed to the ideas at an alternative educators' conference.

• A successful businessman decided that the most important contribution he could make was to invest his time and money in founding a chain of the best possible prep schools. He decided to begin on the West Coast, an area he considered to be in need of such a school, but eventually became disenchanted with the idea of an excellent prep school. He tumbled across information about Sudbury Valley through a speech by John Gatto, and that set him going in this direction.

- A couple in the same state were trying to form a school with home-schooling friends. They realized that each family's ideas about what they wanted were different, and gave up the project until someone introduced them to the Sudbury model through *Free at Last*, which was just what their family had been looking for.

- A woman near the nation's capital, who had been enchanted by Summerhill in college, and who was a very disenchanted teacher, was told to look into Sudbury Valley by a friend. After getting a Press List, she decided she wanted to learn as much as she could and ordered a Planning Kit, which enthralled both her and her husband with the idea of starting this kind of school.

- The husband's brother, equally unhappy with the choice of schools in his area in the Southwest, got turned on to the model after a night-long conversation with the East Coast couple while vacationing with them.

Generally the very beginnings of these groups involve only one or two (in one case, three) people; we will call these people the "ur-founders". It is the task of these people to find others who are willing to participate with them in the work of founding a school. The act of seeking those other participants is in fact the first concrete step towards founding a school.

How founding groups get formed

The first step is for the ur-founder(s) to network among friends, family and acquaintances in the hopes of finding other people that are enthusiastic about the ideas:

> I talked to probably three of my colleagues actively, about what I had seen and heard from Sudbury. I might have talked with friends from high school, and I talked to my family.

> I just would talk to anybody who would talk about it. I ordered books and I would loan them to anybody who would read them. And I loaned the tapes to anybody. It's a small town.

> We started talking to everybody we knew, and spread the word that way. That's how we got started. It's a very interesting concept, and some people do kind of want to talk about it. So it got spread. It took a while, but then the phone started ringing, and people whom neither my wife nor I had talked to started calling about the school. It was a big milestone when that happened.

> Our girls were in a play group already, so there were some people who were interested enough in education to do something different. We thought they might have a 'Eureka' thing like we did. So we got together with some friends and

families that we were used to being with, families that had little ones too.

This phase can take anywhere from a few weeks to a year. Indeed, looking for other founders among acquaintances may or may not be fruitful, and inevitably is followed by "coming out": using public avenues to find others. The variety of such public avenues is enormous, and relates in each case to the interests and talents of the ur-founders. One relatively common method is posting flyers for some sort of meeting in public places and/or mass-mailing flyers to some sort of list.

I put these two page things everywhere and I would get phone calls. We also had them in our office. I don't think I got anybody involved that wasn't off the flyer initially.

I was sending out little brochures and putting in little ads [everywhere]. I had been involved in the voucher movement and the Libertarian Party. I started holding meetings in my house. I sent out postcards to everybody who I had previously sent brochures to.

I made up flyers, got them around town for a couple weeks, posted them, talked to people and handed them out. Talked to all my friends, 'Can you pass it on to somebody else who might be interested?' and so on. The first meeting was in a municipal building, in a hall.

Our neighbor had the mailing list from a food co-op she had in her house. There was also a home-school mailing list that we got hold of. And then we started creating one of our own. We put all these together—over 300 names—and then we sent out a cover letter with a school proposal (a one sheet thing) of what we wanted to do, and announced four public meeting dates.

My friend came over to my house and we started making phone calls. Within a few weeks we had a list of a couple of hundred people who we were contacting and we got the ball rolling right away. Like horses at the race track, just leaping out of their little thing. Going as fast we could.

One rather unusual method of spreading the word resulted in adding two founding families to a group:

*The person who was taking care of my son slipped an article from **Mothering** in my diaper bag one day. She said, "I slipped in an article about a school. There's a woman here in town that is starting a school based on this philosophy." I said, "Yeah, okay" and semi-ignored it, but then that night after getting everybody to bed, I read it. It rang so true, it just hit me in the heart.*

The purpose of going public is to establish a broad-based founding group. The mechanism is almost always through a series of meetings of one sort or another: social gatherings, discussions about education, lectures, showings of videos. At each of these meetings appeals are made to individual attendees who might be interested in working seriously towards founding a school.

The frequency of these meetings can vary from weekly to monthly to erratically, often depending on the particular stage of development of the group. Sometimes a meeting is held and *no one* new comes, which can be very discouraging. The key to success seems to be persistence. Sometimes the beginnings can be especially difficult.

*If they'd had ripe tomatoes, they would have thrown them at me. Three adults and three kids came to my first meeting at one of our branch libraries. I showed the "Intro to Sudbury Valley" video, plus the BBC segment of "Sudbury on TV". That's what got 'em riled. The fact smoking was allowed. Plus the F-word (bleeped out). One woman who was there with her 10-year-old daughter said she was "horrified" and she would never send her daughter to such a school. (The reasons this woman came: she'd seen my letter to the editor, the school sounded like Montessori where she teaches **and** she thought she was coming to hear another person with the same name as mine, a paraplegic (some local kid I'd never heard of who graduated from high school after accomplishing great things despite his handicaps). The second woman was offended by Danny's comment that kids deserve to be treated with the same respect as adults ("kids ARE different than adults" she said, and what if they wanted to bring a gun to school, or have sex, or take drugs? I told her no illegal activities are allowed, but that didn't calm her.) The third woman had studied and supported Summerhill and so she spent the rest of the time arguing with the other two. It was not a sterling beginning. But it was a beginning.*

My first thought: I should not have shown the BBC video. On second thought, maybe I should always show it. Won't that separate the wheat from the chaff very quickly, and save everybody a lot of time? If they're going to get sidetracked or put off by that few seconds of the video, by the smoking issue, I figure they'd never be able to support lots of the other key parts of the SVS philosophy. But maybe I'm wrong. I think you have to be 18 to buy cigarettes in Florida, which I gather is not true in Massachusetts, so maybe I should've talked about smoking from the legal angle, and reminded them Massachusetts has different laws, and that rules are passed by School Meeting, so if smoking were legal and you were against it, you would get to have your say.

*The most discouraging thing was the poor turnout. Seems few people respond to fliers and even fewer to letters to the editor calling for a new school. On a brighter note, one of the kids was a 12-year-old boy who had been in my son's fifth-grade class when he was still in public school. The kid just happened to be at the library, working as a volunteer. He asked me what my meeting was about. I explained very briefly the school's philosophy and he immediately went to the phone to call his mother to see if she could attend the meeting. She couldn't. But he sat through the video and all the heated discussions. I gave him a copy of the **Learning Without Coercion** article. Everything he heard about SVS struck a strong chord. It gave me hope.*

At some point the public meetings are continued as avenues for widening exposure to the school's ideas and eventually getting supporters, students and also staff members. Meanwhile the founders coalesce into a working group to which people are added (often as result of attending informational public meetings) and from which people drop out as they realize they are either not interested in doing the work or cannot support the ideas.

We had an informational meeting once a month to introduce new people to the idea, showing a videotape, talking, having refreshments. We had founding group meetings every two weeks. We started off with about a dozen people. The second meeting had a different dozen. By the third founding group meeting, we had four people, and we stayed at four for months.

In order to actually get a school going, it seems that the ur-founders have to supplement their number with at least half a dozen or so others. However, it is not realistic to think that the work will be shared equally among these founders. Usually the ur-founders end up doing the lion's share of the work; occasionally they are lucky enough to find another one or two people as committed as they are.

Characteristics important within the founding group

A founding group has a great many specific tasks to perform as it goes about getting a school going. Many skills are needed, but it seems to be true that very few of them have to be available within the group: most specialized activities can be carried out through friends, acquaintances and professionals that the group chooses to work with. Thus, for example, legal work, bookkeeping, graphic arts, and the construction trades can be farmed out if necessary; and realtors are central to finding a site.

There are however several features that a founding group must possess. There has to be a central core of people—at least one or two—that holds the vision of what the group is setting out to do; in other words, a core that has a clear understanding of the model and, withstanding all pressure, continues to hold the intention. Usually, this has involved buying a Planning Kit, amassing literature to share with others, and becoming quite familiar with the contents of this literature. Almost always, it also involves a visit to a Sudbury school, which can often be an intensely emotional experience.

> *After five minutes of walking in, I was in tears. It was very moving, and I remember punching S. in the arm saying, "Damn, you knew when you brought me here this was going to happen! You knew it! Alright, alright, I'm on board."*

Although a knowledgeable core group with a consistent philosophy is a *sine qua non* for establishing a school with a clearly articulated model, it is also clear that as time goes on, members of the founding group will deepen their understanding of the model.

The one thing that I think was incredibly difficult, looking back, is that we were "coming" to Sudbury Valley. We were all entranced by it; we couldn't stop talking about it, we were just thinking about every aspect of our lives. But we were coming to it at different levels. We were coming to it slowly. There was one point that was kind of an immediate flash, and we were like "aha!", but after that we were working out the details.

What happened with the three of us that was really hard, and I think it was very good, is that one person would get there and all of a sudden they would see the light. And they would argue passionately. And the other two would be really resisting. Or else two people would get to this point. So we would go through these endless arguments, just a drag-down fight. So two of us would be defending this, or couldn't agree, and we'd be arguing, arguing, arguing. We were going through these incredible internal struggles. We would just argue with each other until it became apparent we all agreed. Then all of a sudden it wouldn't be an issue, we'd all kind of say, "Oh, yeah, ok." But in the meantime we were presenting this united front to the parents. We just felt we have to do this, or the whole thing's going to crumble. So we'd be sitting in these meetings and say, well, "you know, we all really buy this line, we all agree," while one of us would have just arrived the night before. And adamantly defended it the next day.

So there was that level of it. And then there was the level where we were really trying to work out what we were going to do. For a while we'd say to parents, "We're not Sudbury Valley. We buy this and this and this and this, but we're not Sudbury Valley." So there were these three levels. There was the level among us: where are we? What do we really believe? There was this level of presenting a united front to parents: "we believe this, and this is what you parents should see us all believing." And then there was this level: "where are we going to end up? Where do we really want to go with this? What are we ultimately going to agree on?" It was an incredibly stressful time. I remember being so paranoid at every meeting that something I said wouldn't be agreed upon in the group. So we'd say some things. And then two people would be glaring at you. It was like, "oh, shit; I'm not supposed to say that."

*I remember a parent talking about the fishing story in **Free at Last**. I was saying, "oh yeah, we totally believe that." I remember thinking, "I can't look at the other two, because I can't remember what everyone else believes right now." And I remember thinking, "I wonder if they're going to die when this is over, if they'll go 'what the heck—do you think I believe that? I don't buy that story!'" And that was kind of where we were always, someone would say something and the others would go, "I didn't know we were there."*

So we'd go back to processing time after that. The public meetings would be really stormy—we all had ulcers from that—but then we'd have processing time afterwards, and it was like, "well you said this, and we didn't agree with this—I can't believe you said that."

*It was a very schizoid time; it's like, "where are we?
Where is our solid ground here?" It just felt really, really
difficult. And it went on for two years!*

Indeed, some members of the founding group as they
deepen their understanding, will also increase their misgiv-
ings about it, and drop by the wayside.

*We were quite near; school was going to start in the
fall. Late in the spring, H. started talking about wanting to have stuff in place. That was a real difference
right there. He thought people couldn't handle it if they
didn't have structure to start with. In fact, we really
started with a blank slate. We had some problems later,
but I never questioned doing it that way. That was a
real major philosophic issue between him and the rest
of us that foreshadowed, I think, what happened [later,
when he ultimately withdrew].*

Another essential feature is that there be someone or
ones among the founders who have the time and energy
to make what is basically an entrepreneurial commitment
without limits—namely, a commitment to do whatever has
to be done in order to establish the institution. It is impossible to exaggerate the amount or the difficulty of the work
it takes to get a school like this started. Every piece along
the way is much more difficult than it would be if one were
starting a more traditional school. Everybody involved in
the establishment of the school, from officials to trades-
people to real estate agents to neighbors to parents to students, have to be "brought on board" laboriously; that is,
they have to be walked through descriptions of the model
(which may be counter-intuitive to them) until they understand it enough to participate in its creation, however

centrally or peripherally. It is not unusual for the burden to be too great for even energetic and committed founders to bear. This is especially the case when the number of people doing almost all of the work is very small, say one or two.

There have been times of great frustration with the process because there is so much ticky-tack work to do, and a lot of it has really fallen upon two of us. Personally, I got tired of talking about why it is such a good idea. I used to be able to talk about it until four in the morning, and now I want more people to understand that this is the best idea there is in schools. Sometimes I feel like I want to give it up and move away really quickly, like tomorrow, and live in a village where there aren't any schools.

Someone in the founding group (hopefully more than one person) has to be a good organizer. With countless things to do, the entropic tendency towards chaos easily predominates without the presence of a determined source of order. Otherwise, meetings are unbearable, public events never even happen, lists don't get made, mailings don't go out, official papers aren't filed in a timely manner, bills aren't paid, inquiries aren't followed up, promotional materials aren't created, etc. While it is true that much of the routine administrative work can be done by volunteers or hired labor under supervision, the group itself must include people with the ability to see the whole picture, to analyze it into constituent parts, to define the sequence of actions to be taken and the time frames in which they must be achieved.

The importance of another characteristic in members of a founding group can scarcely be overemphasized, although it is occasionally absent: the ability to hold an audience, whether the audience be a family, a roomful of people, or "just" the fire inspector. One might call this "presence", coupled with the ability to communicate one's thoughts in a simple, coherent, and concise fashion, both in speech and in writing. Effective communication is the starting point for conveying the ideas of the model to the uninitiated, and also in attracting that small percentage of people who are already predisposed to the concepts. Lacking the ability to communicate well, a group must depend on people—both founders and others—coming to the school pretty much on their own steam. This presents a serious obstacle and is liable to cripple the efforts of the group.

One of the most desirable features of a founding group is the one that is almost always lacking: agreement among its members on their educational goals, in particular on the meaning of the Sudbury model. In this regard a founder had the following to say:

> *The first advice I always have is that there IS going to be a split if you have more than three people, or even with three people, and those people should be invited to form their own school. Make it happen as fast and as early as you can.*

Perhaps the main reason people with varying views come in the first place is expressed here:

> *I think part of the reason why a lot of the families couldn't stick it out with our school is because they were so desperately looking for "something else" that it didn't matter specifically what it was. Just "something else".*

At any rate, having a founding group with a clear consensus on where it is going is a highly desirable but seldom attainable goal.

Concrete steps each group must take:

- *Understanding and explaining the philosophy*

One way or another, every group must figure out specific ways to achieve two goals. The first is to deepen the understanding members of the founding group have of the model; and the second is to find ways to help others (parents, the public) grasp what this highly unfamiliar method of education is about.

It seems that pretty much every group organizes sessions, or meetings, open to the public, and designed to explain the ideas of the school. Most groups hold these sessions on a fairly regular schedule for some period of time: it may be every week or every other week for a few months, or it may be monthly for years. The sessions feature either a discussion of a subject, a presentation followed by questions and answers, showing videos, or discussing books together. Some of the founders, including some who are articulate and are fairly advanced in their understanding of the Sudbury model, must be present at each session. For the founders themselves, articulating the ideas deepens their mastery of them, and offers opportunities to enrich and elaborate them.

Fairly typical is the following:

> *This is an update on my efforts to start an SVS-type school here. I've held six "public meetings". For several of those meetings, no one showed up. For most of the others, only one or two people. At last Monday's meeting, 7:10 rolled around and I started up the "Intro to Sudbury Valley" video. Four*

*people were there. I thought "Hot dog! Four people!" I
dimmed the lights and two more people straggled in.
Then two or three more. And two or three more. I was
having to hustle up chairs! Total count was 15 by the
time the lights came up, not counting me. I felt as if
I were in the movie Field of Dreams, "build it and
they will come". I hadn't built anything, but they were
coming anyway!*

*Where did they all come from? Two had seen a post-
er at the Civic Media Center. One had heard about
it from a friend who had seen the video earlier after
reading a poster at the library. Two women came from
90 miles away after reading an article I'd written in
an environmental publication here. One woman saw
my 1x1-inch ad in the local paper. Another woman and
her sister had read another article I wrote in a local
New Age publication. A couple heard about it from a
neighbor who had just moved to the area who heard
about it from they didn't know where. A second couple
had found a flier on their car (one of few responses I've
received from my "experiment" putting about 500 fliers
on cars during church services. I received one call from
an irate elderly man berating me for "desecrating" his
place of worship.) In short, everything I've done is reap-
ing rewards in small ways that seem to be slowly adding
up.*

*What's more, the group immediately asked some
"hard" questions. One woman asked if parents would
be allowed to spend as much time at the school as they
wanted. I said no and elaborated as best I could about
why not. Another person asked if the school would allow a kid to watch tv all day, if he so chose. I said yes,*

and talked about world views and I can't remember what else. Bottom line, no one walked out! In fact, they signed up their names, addresses and phone numbers to receive information about my next meeting.

I had already planned a meeting at my house for two days later for what I thought would be two or three people who earlier had expressed more solid interest in playing some part in helping establish the school. These were people who had read a couple of the books already, had seen another video and maybe even listened to a couple of audiotapes. I assumed this meeting would be the first of ongoing "study" sessions, to acquaint these people more deeply with the philosophy. Instead of three people showing up, there were six. And three or four others have said they want to be at the next meeting. (We've tentatively agreed to meet every two weeks through the summer.)

I suspect these people have varying degrees of "tolerance" for the details of how things really work at SVS, depending on how wholeheartedly they are leaning toward wanting to be a founder. My goal, as I see it, is to try to present the reality of SVS . . .

Getting attendance at these meetings is perhaps the most difficult task. Most groups quickly build mailing lists of people whom they hope will have even the slightest interest, and they mail assiduously to these lists. Often, lists are built from friends, acquaintances, people involved in other ventures (e.g., food co-ops or political action groups) with a founder, people who have made inquiries already, friends of friends, educators, guidance counselors, etc. More random approaches have to be tried too in order to widen the range of people from which an audience might be collected. For example, flyers can be posted and/or distributed in libraries, supermarkets, medical offices, public buildings, day care centers, public bulletin boards, coffee houses, etc. Computer bulletin boards may have some usefulness. Special mailing lists can be obtained, usually by purchase, such as local subscriber lists to various "green" publications, local newspapers aimed at parental or educational concerns, etc. Where to hold the meetings is another question that must be answered. Besides the obvious venue of a private home (a stressful situation under the best of circumstances) or of the school site, if it exists already, most communities have public meeting facilities in libraries or in other public buildings that are either free or very inexpensive.

There are subjects that come up over and over in meetings to acquaint people with the philosophy of the school, as well as in meetings of founders working on getting a school started. All of them have been discussed—over and over again, in all sorts of ways—in various publications and in tapes in the Planning Kit. One can depend upon discussing these topics many different times, and losing some people along the way who earlier had seemed interested and maybe even committed. These polarizing issues include:

- exposure: "How is it possible for a child to get an education if adults do not expose them to various things they need to know?" [Through their insatiable natural curiosity, of course.]

- forced learning (curriculum): "I would never have known I was interested in playing the piano if my parents hadn't forced me to do it when I was a child; now, it is an important part of my life." [Maybe you would be enjoying painting, or skiing, if you had been able to make your own choices.]

- cultural literacy: "How can we ensure that our culture will survive if we don't see to it that young people learn its essential components?" [We can't anyway, unless the culture has enough inherent value to be worthy of passionate interest on its own merits.]

- safety: "Isn't it dangerous for little children to be unsupervised? And isn't it dangerous for little children to be around older, more aggressive children?" The passions in this discussion rise even further when the subject moves to the next logical extension: the open campus. [Yes, it is dangerous; but more dangerous for children to be supervised and constantly studying how to escape their supervision. Allowing children to develop judgment and self-confidence enhances the odds of survival.]

- age mixing: "I don't want my young child exposed to discussions about sex, drugs, and other subjects that interest teenagers." [Put him/her in a box.]

- governance: "How can kids choose their teachers? How can they make judgments about right and wrong among their peers? How can they be expected to manage the day to day affairs of an institution?" [There is no evidence that kids are any worse at these tasks than anyone else, and there is lots of evidence by now that they are competent.]

In addition, each group usually manages to develop their own specific obsessions. Some worry about gender bias, others about diversity, and still others about afford-ability.

The most important thing is to keep discussing these and other issues that occupy the attention of the group, be-cause whatever the topic, these discussions invariably hark back to the basic principles underlying the school. Through these debates and clashes, the principles become clarified, strengthened, and defined in the minds of the audience and the founders.

It is also, however, important not to get totally bogged down on issues that have been discussed to death by al-most all of the group members but still are not settled in the minds of a few. There have been groups that have been mired for months in the debate about open campus to the detriment (even exclusion) of other questions members wanted to address. One founder recalls:

> One of my contributions, via a friend, was: "Don't let other people use your meetings to talk about their pet ideas." That's one of the best pieces of advice we ever had in the whole process. The group, at my urging, took the stance: "Well, of course, there's lots of room for reform, and that's an interesting idea, but that's not what we're doing here." We had a number of times when people came for one meeting to try to talk their pet theory. We rebuffed them; they went away. It saved us a lot of non-sense.

Concrete steps each group must take
• *Formalization of status*

In the beginning, the ur-founders and the people who begin to work with them usually just carry on pursuing their goals. There is a lot of work to do, not very many people to do it, and everyone is thrilled that it gets done at all. The controversial decisions that have to be made are usually ironed out in informal discussions. Meanwhile, the group may be growing a little bit, and as it grows and gets more determined to get a school going, the need to introduce some structure becomes clear to everybody. The reason for this is that the number and complexity of the decisions increases significantly as the reality of the school looms. It becomes important to distinguish who should be accepted into the decision-making circle, and what mechanism should be used to formalize decisions. Indeed, there comes a point when the people who have been working hard are not necessarily ready to share equally in the decision-making with every newcomer.

For some groups, the transition to a formal "founding group" happens smoothly and almost casually. In one instance, "the structure of the founding group was anybody who came. Decisions were made hopefully by consensus." At the other extreme are groups that introduce strict criteria very early on for becoming a founder. Here are two examples:

> *We welcome anyone to our meetings. However, the only participants who can vote are founders. To become a*

founder, a person must participate in meetings (not all, but most) for two consecutive months and demonstrate an understanding of the school philosophy (having read an SVS Press book can indicate this). When we created these criteria, all the founding members became founders. Since that time, we have elected two others. Although we have had people join us for a while and then leave, none have commented that they felt misled or resentful. Rather, it looks like they became informed enough about the school's philosophy to decide it is not for them. Which is as it should be.

Creating a formal founding group also helped us clarify the purposes to different meetings: . . . we designated our bi-monthly founding meetings to be work and task oriented.

Our founding group met weekly for almost a year before we opened. We did run purely introductory events as well, but mainly we would loan or sell new people a book and invite them to come to a founders' meeting. We'd take a few minutes at the beginning for them to introduce themselves, and then get on with business. You can always talk individually afterwards. Here are the requirements we had for becoming a founder:

1) Attend two consecutive founding meetings. These meetings are open to non-founders who have satisfied 2) below.

2) Read "Free at Last" or "The Sudbury Valley Experience" or watch the video interview with Dan Greenberg.

3) Be committed to make [our school] happen in the Sudbury model.

4) Be committed to ongoing self-education about the Sudbury philosophy as it applies to [our school].
5) Pay accumulated fee to treasury.
6) A founder's status will lapse if s/he misses two consecutive meetings or does not pay assessed dues by the meeting following the assessment. Lapsed founders cannot vote. Lapsed founders can be reinstated at the beginning of the second consecutive meeting attended (if they lapsed because of non-attendance), reading minutes of missed meetings, and paying all back fees.

An important aspect of the formalization phase is establishing what the decision making process will be. The process adopted in the founding group may also affect the way decisions are made in the school once the school has opened. Most groups have opted for a standard, majority-rule voting procedure, operating under some sub-set of *Robert's Rules of Order*. Others have preferred a form of consensus governance up until the moment of opening the school. To date, once open, every operating school has chosen the former method for its School Meetings. Interestingly, however, the reality of School Meetings usually involves debating every issue until the members come to agree on a resolution; a matter is generally only put to a vote when all viewpoints have been thoroughly aired, and there is not likelihood that differences can be resolved. Sometimes the founding groups can become highly structured, as in the following example:

Meeting Structure

Special Meetings—Like committee meetings may be called when necessary and scheduled when most convenient. Like committee meetings, proposals must be brought to a regular meeting to be voted upon in order to be adopted.

Quorum—nothing can be decided by majority vote unless the majority consists of at least four founders. This means that business may be transacted by as few as four founders present and voting at a regular meeting if they are all in agreement.

Check-in—members can say what they want or need to feel "present" and can speak for 30 seconds or less. There is no discussion or response to check-in.

Announcements—5 minutes or less total. Can be added to agenda at this time.

Minutes; reading, correction and approval—7 minutes or less

Agenda—Items which should appear on the agenda, but were inadvertently dropped out by the Chair in forming the agenda mailed with the minutes may be added by majority vote. The Chair is responsible for keeping track of what should appear on the agenda. Founders please help by contacting the Chair as soon as they realize something they expected to see on the agenda is not there—5 minutes or less.

Committee reports—10 minutes each. Give an overview of the committee's progress on its various projects to the whole group but do not include presentation or discussion of new proposals.

Old business—includes any second or later readings of written proposals and discussion followed by vote. Minor amendments can be made, if this can be accomplished within the time limit, same as new proposals below. A majority vote is required to adopt the proposal, to reject it entirely or to send it back for further re-working and another reading.

New business—New proposals. Any first reading of a proposal must be brought in writing, read to the meeting, and given to the Secretary to include in the minutes. Ten minutes discussion will be allotted in which time minor amendments may be proposed and adopted. The proposal as amended may be adopted by vote at this time. If the discussion reveals that major amendments are required (i.e., more extensive than can be accomplished in the time limit) the proposal will be returned to committee for re-working and brought back to a later meeting at which time it will be considered "old business". Also, if any founder requests a second reading to allow more time for consideration, then the proposal will be discussed but not voted on, and will be brought for discussion and/or vote at the following meeting as old business.

Brief items—up to 10 minutes allowed. The President may prioritize and schedule items presented to him/her in writing under this topic right up to meeting time. This is primarily to allow us to expedite simple and urgent proposals generated by committees during the week (after the agenda deadline.) and other minor matters at the President's discretion. If a brief item cannot be voted upon within the time limit allowed for it, it can come up at the next meeting under Old Business.

Adjournment—includes announcement of next meeting date and time.

At some point every founding group finally incorporates[1]; some do it very early on, others not until they are essentially ready to open. Some groups do it themselves, using laymen's guides to incorporation, while most use the services of an attorney. To date, every school has incorporated as a not-for-profit corporation, although several considered becoming a for-profit entity. The benefits of the former status include: exemption from state and local taxes, and from federal taxes on income (although all organizations have to contribute various federal payroll taxes); tax exemptions for donors of gifts and money; and eligibility for various private and governmental grants and loans that are offered only to not-for-profit institutions. For-profit status looses all tax preferences, but allows for the distribution of net profits (if any) in any manner that the corporation wishes.

---

[1] Several groups in recent years have tried, unsuccessfully, to establish Charter Schools similar to the Sudbury model, within the framework of the public school system. Every state has different regulations governing Charter Schools, but all appear to have one thing in common: Charter Schools must always include specific academic objectives and systems of assessment that severely restrict the degree of freedom to experiment with innovative educational ideas. Similar restrictions apply to voucher systems under consideration to date, insofar as they determine what schools will be eligible to receive vouchers. Until these restrictions are removed, there is little reason to expect that a Sudbury school can be founded within any public education framework.

Not-for-profit status can only be obtained by filing specific papers with the Internal Revenue Service. (Once the IRS grants the application, it is usually a relatively simple matter to file an application with state and local authorities, which usually follow suit without delay.) Some schools begin operating without having gained not for profit status, but it generally is sensible to take care of it in advance of opening. Again, some groups file papers on their own without help, and others have legal and accounting help for this process. The fact is that the ease with which various IRS offices grant this status varies from place to place and from official to official.

Part of the process of incorporation involves the drafting of Corporate By-Laws. Most schools have modeled their by-laws on those of Sudbury Valley, which are included in the Planning Kit that the SVS Press distributes. Many schools have been willing to share their By-Laws with others. Some variations relate to the laws of various states; others to the design of the group.

Regardless of the detailed nature of the by-laws, all must address the following issues:

- the purposes of the Corporation: this is an opportunity for each group to formulate a concise mission statement that will give focus to all the group's activities.

- the role of parents: each school must decide whether and to what extent to include parents of students in decision making processes.

- the role of the School Meeting (students and staff combined): each group has to define the range of powers granted legally to the School Meeting.

In addition, either the by-laws or some other legal document (e.g., the minutes of a formal meeting of members of the Corporation, however they are defined) must make some provision for the transition from a founding state to a state of operation as a school. For example, neither formally enrolled students, nor parents of enrolled students, exist before the school is open, a fact that must be taken into account during the transition period when considering how to carry out the functions of the Assembly and/or School Meeting.

Concrete steps each group must take:

- *Satisfying the appropriate educational authorities*

It is impossible to imagine how diverse different states' rules and regulations are regarding the freedom to found private schools. In some cases, the existence of any private school is effectively, if not legally, entirely under the jurisdiction of a local town, or city, school board. This means that the ability to found a Sudbury school can vary from location to location within a single state! In other cases, private schools come directly under state jurisdiction, and the state may have very little, or very much, to say about how the school operates educationally.

Here is an example of a situation which is a "walk in the park":

> *You just file an affidavit with the state saying that you're a private school. You need to list curriculums, but it's really easy. They tell you what curriculum is required, and all they require is that you offer those things. And we do offer all those things. . .*

Here's another walk in the park—perhaps twice around the park in this case:

> *To be recognized as a school for attendance you have to basically state your intention and a few more things. In the beginning we did have a stickling with one thing. We have to have quarterly assessments "as appropriate". So we said to ourselves, it's never appropriate. That's actually legitimate*

in our case. We felt entirely comfortable saying that. But there had to be a written report. And so about four times a year we send letters saying we're going to have a potluck, etc. And in that letter we always say, "The kids are doing great." Every year, we just send the state the same letter saying, "We've done it". And nobody cares, really.

Then we have an example of a group that had to jump through some uncomfortable hoops, but in the end managed to make it:

When we first went to the Department of Education, the Department of Academics, with our offering in hand, their first reaction was, "No. This won't work." And I'm pretty sure that what they really thought was we would just fold our hands and go away. The thing was such a huge amount of work, I think they thought, "We'll just say 'no', and they'll just disappear."

The state said you have to have a planned course. And, frankly, we put it together. Working on it was one of the worst periods of my life. We had to work on it after school opened, because they told us the week before. It took hours and hours and hours and hours in the evenings and on weekends when I was just physically exhausted. We were reeling from school all day, and had to come home every night and face hours of this really boring, stupid, valueless work. It's awful. We opened without official permission, but we were in process. And they never said, "Do not open."[2]

And then we have an example of the little engine that couldn't, no matter how hard it tried.

I called the State in the fall of '94, and they sent a letter saying in order to get a certificate of approval, these are the steps that you have to go through. I knew it was bad news right then. They sent a copy of the code and I looked through it and we decided that the curriculum and the system of credits are the two things that would not get us approved. By June we officially discovered that was true. So, anyway, we had this dialogue with the State that had begun in the fall.

From January until June, I said, "This is not going to work. The curriculum and system of credits will not work," but others said, "We can finesse it. We can do it. We'll just be positive about this." Then, of course, come June, it didn't work. So we wasted all sorts of energy. It brought our group closer together, I know, but it was like shared misery, putting together this huge package for the State.

---

[2]Actually, this particular case is a little more complicated. In the beginning, the school did in fact present some of the planned curriculum it had prepared. It took a few years for the founders to realize that by doing so they had compromised their original dream. When they restructured their school to the Sudbury model, they were able to continue functioning, albeit with a certain degree of anxiety regarding the state's reaction to their new program.

In April, the State Committee of the founding group went up to the Capital and met with the accreditation specialist who was assigned our case. In advance of our visit, by about a month, we sent our documents and a copy of **Free at Last** *and also a copy of* **Legacy of Trust.** *One of the documents that we sent was very much like, "If the child wants to learn English, these are the things that could happen." That was our curriculum. And it was very well worded. We sent these materials and four of us, all teachers or former teachers, went up because we thought, "How can we lose with this team? We know all the jargon, all the buzz words, blah, blah, blah." When we got there it was immediately clear that they hadn't even read the materials we sent, hadn't even flipped through anything. I literally saw the woman flipping through a book before we got to the meeting. It was just amazing levels of incompetence. We thought it would work. But it didn't. They thought it was a methodology, not a curriculum. We wouldn't be able to get away with this. We had to be much more detailed.*

We sat down and talked about it some. All four of us left with the impression that what she told us to do is to write a curriculum and don't use it. There was another part of it too. The system of credits just didn't come up again. One of us wondered, "What about the system of credits?" But the rest of us felt, "No, no, it's fine." And so that became our strategy pretty quickly. We're going to do this bogus curriculum, and just put it in and not use it. We were elated. Great, we're going to be able to do this with the State. The deadline was June 13th, so of course the first two weeks in June were absolute bedlam around here because we were trying to put together this excessive package of information. Literally, how many math manipulatives you have by each grade, etc. Our basement is full of books and manipulatives. If anybody wants a manipulative, help yourself. And textbooks.

It was really weird. Every day or two we would change 180 degrees on something. We had an emergency founders meeting because we got to a point where you had to show grades in order for a child to move from one grade to the next. It wasn't working any way we could put it together. We tried "P" = "participation" in ninth grade; and if you got a "P" that means you have taken the subject. Well, it would have been obvious if a child hadn't taken English, history, science, math and an elective, but we were going to give him a "P" anyway. It just wasn't working. So we had this Founding Member meeting where we said we're going to submit our original curriculum, which they called a methodology back in April and the system of credit with a "P", knowing that they would reject it because we would not compromise our beliefs on anything. All the founders agreed to that, so we bagged all of the curriculum. But we did send in all of our materials because we had them, so why not send them in. We didn't say that we would use them in anything that we sent in. We just listed them. They're all in our basement.

We kind of knew it was going to be rejection. It took over a month for them to get back to us. It was a letter telling us that we should have a much more detailed curriculum and a system of credits. But there was an Orwellian paragraph at the end which said, "We want to remind you that [our state] is very open to educational alternatives, and we really support different kinds of schools, blah, blah, blah," after this very detailed letter budging not an inch from their original position on anything, really. So that was the State.

This group eventually had to attempt a completely novel way of getting around the state's limitations. [3]

The moral of the story is that it is important for any founding group to get to know, as early as possible, what its options are, and to plan a strategy from the outset. Several groups that have not done so have failed either before they began or early in their operation.

---

[3] They essentially founded a secular church, hoping to remove state supervision by taking advantage of the doctrine of separation of church and state. As of this writing, the verdict is still out on this attempt.

Concrete steps each group must take:

- *Money matters*

The amount of start-up money required to get a school going varies so much from group to group, and from location to location, that no generalizations can be made. At one extreme lie schools that got going with a total of only a very few thousand dollars, and relied on the first year's tuition to provide operating funds from the minute the doors opened. At the other extreme lie founding groups that, one way or another, had access to significant assets—in the form of cash, or real estate, or both—which gave them the freedom to experiment, and lowered the anxiety about initial enrollment. Here are two examples of schools that started on shoestrings:

> *Where did the money come from? [The two ur-founders] paid for the postage and things. Before school started, we spent probably $800 or so. For phone, and flyers, supplies, postage, and ads and copies. Hundreds of copies were made at home on a copy machine. The founders weren't assessed, nobody was assessed. Tuition for the first year was a way to get some money for startup costs. That was what started up the bankbook. And we had a yard sale for $200; and bottles: we really nickel-and-dimed it.*

> *In the beginning of the group, I think maybe people just kind of gave five bucks or ten bucks here or something to just help cover whatever had been spent. And then when*

we formalized, [two ur-founders] made a sizeable contribution, around $1,500. We also took contributions from others—several thousand dollars from one family, much of it in up-front tuition for the first year. Expenses for the first two years of the group, before the school started, were pretty small. Periodically the founders would all kick in about fifty dollars. And also we had a home copier to do all of our leaflet copying and flyer copying. People still donate a lot, little things, like virtually all the paper products the school has ever had: toilet paper, paper towels, and even brochures. For instance, one founder would print up a hundred brochures and just pay for it—wouldn't take it out of the school's budget, that type of thing.

Tuition money in the spring before opening provided start-up funds as well as a little extra pressure to go through with opening—"God, now we're taking people's money!"

Here is an example of a school somewhere between the extremes, both in the amount of funds available and in the security that having funds gave the founders to concentrate on their other work:

The business meeting members voted: "Capital campaign authorized". I don't have the exact wording here, but the capital campaign consisted of non-secured founders' loan notes, in the total amount of $20,000. Interest would be determined by the person who was giving us the money, up to 6%. Some were for 0%, some for 2%, 3%, and the largest chunk was for $12,000 at 6%, which we are now in the process of paying back. That turned into an ugly scene when the lender's friend *left the school. There's nothing free. But that person is making 6% on their money, which is greater than they would get in the bank right now. We may have gotten a few donations, too, but it was basically our money.*

What I remember is the transition from a study group with no commitment and no money to me checking that these were people with good anti-bias politics, and that they were willing to all put some money in the pot. There are a number of places where I would have said "I'm in the wrong place," one of which would have been people not willing to get real in the sense that putting money in the pot represents getting real. We charged ourselves a membership fee of $100 apiece. That's not very much, but it is enough to drive away people who want to sit in somebody's living room and "talk ideas". It brought a speaker out from the East Coast.

We eventually set up a payment schedule for the founders' notes. The Assembly said, "we're going to do this much this year, this much next year." We set up sort of a five year plan to pay those back. People who lent us money varied from being "ok, keep it as long as you want," to the woman who threatened to sue, and came to an Assembly meeting to talk about it and never said a word.

I talked to several lawyers during that time to see what our responsibility was, and what recourse people had. Basically everybody said, "if you don't have any money, then you can't get blood from a stone. You need to try to be responsible, figure out a payment plan, present it to these people, but what are they going to do? There's no money there." So that's what we did. We set up some sort of long-term payment plan for that money, which we're still doing.

And then there is the other extreme:

I had this worry that basically we'd have three kids, or two kids, or four kids or something. Fortunately we had the money, and that was a big, big difference. The fact is that we were going to be here, regardless of whether we had two or twenty. We had the money because I had made a bunch of money. Period.

We had brochures, the first three different versions. We passed out 2,000 flyers. We have a description of the school in probably a dozen various on-line forums here or there. We have a home page. We sold lots of books. We're running ads. We're probably the foremost advertiser of any Sudbury Valley type school. We know what works and what doesn't work there. We spent a great deal of effort on these ads. And they did have a beneficial effect, although most of the money was wasted. But still, what was not wasted was very productive.

Before the school opened, the facilities committee was getting this place ready. It was finding furniture, rehabbing furniture. Everything big was begged from friends and neighbors. Or found on the street and overhauled—from a fridge to bookshelves to the copier. The total cost of everything in the school, including the sign and the bookshelves, which are our two big expenditures, was about $1,300, because we had serious scroungers out there. And some generous people.

There have probably been three dozen attempts to start schools like ours, and [maybe] two dozen of them washed out, or they still haven't gotten out of the box.

And we did it. What did we do that made a difference between us and the people that haven't gotten out of the box? One thing was money. The fact that we didn't have to worry about where are we going to find the starting $50,000. We had a building already locked up because we had money. It's not just the money, it's that we didn't have to worry about it. It's the fact that what I'm sure must have been one of the biggest concerns of other groups when they were starting up, we didn't really spend that much time thinking about. And so we were able to spend our time doing other stuff. Money isn't the only key success factor, but if you have it, it makes success a lot easier.

Whatever the differences in acquiring seed money, the first year budgets for new schools are remarkably similar to one another. They are thin on disbursements to staff, economical on materials and equipment, and frugal on other basic expenses. With time and growth, some slack may finally appear.

In a more nitty-gritty practical vein, a number of steps have to be taken to get a group's fiscal house in order. In general, the earlier these are begun the sooner everyone involved takes the enterprise seriously and considers it a viable venture.

A bank account must be opened. This can be done even before the group is formalized, and needs only a minuscule amount of seed money to start. This immediately gives the group a record of income and expenses and a checkbook. Once the group is formalized, a regular commercial account can be established at a bank.

An initial bookkeeping system has to be established. Once again, this professionalizes the organization's record-keeping from the outset and makes it possible to provide meaningful on-going reports. The Planning Kit contains a sample of the chart of accounts used by Sudbury Valley School in its computerized accounting system. Many groups, and schools in their initial phases, have computerized accounts (for the most part simpler than that now in use at Sudbury Valley); others have similar systems to the one that served Sudbury Valley well for its first 15 years, a manual One-Write system. It is a good idea to get the advice of someone knowledgeable in accounting or book-keeping (or maybe both!) to help establish a system, especially since from the moment when the income creeps over $100,000 a year, certified audits may be required.

It is also important to establish a good filing system and keep records in such a manner that a clean audit trail can easily be found for each transaction. Especially in a management environment such as that of a Sudbury school, where spending decisions are broadly decentralized, it is essential that members of the community have comfortable access to all the information they may need to develop informed opinions about the validity of the expenditures being made.

Concrete steps each group must take:
• *Site selection*

No task has consistently given more heartache and agony to all start-up groups than the task of finding an appropriate site. Many factors go into what makes a site "appropriate":

(1) Accessibility to the population the group seeks to draw upon

The group has to define the locus of its target population as much as it possibly can. This is an important decision, and it may evolve as the group grows and defines itself. Sudbury Valley drew most of its founders and community political support from the town of Framingham, 20 miles west of Boston, and as a result concentrated its efforts on locating within 10 miles of Framingham, and drawing the majority of its students from a radius of about 20 miles of Framingham. Red Cedar School, in Bristol, Vermont (several miles south of the city of Burlington) and Evergreen School, in Gardiner, Maine (slightly south of Augusta) each decided to focus their efforts on the population in and around their small towns rather than shift their center of gravity to the adjacent larger cities. On the other hand, The Circle School, originally located in Lewisberry, Pennsylvania (south of the city of Harrisburg), after about 10 years of operation, decided to relocate to Harrisburg and shift its center of population to that city. There is no formula that is right or wrong; what is important is to know what you are focussing on and to stick to it until forced by circumstances to re-evaluate and change.

A factor always to be considered when thinking about the accessibility issue is the availability of public transportation and the local cultural attitudes toward commuting by car. In certain parts of the country, such as Boston and New York, a commute of an hour or more each way is not considered unusual (although in the former case it is normally done by automobile, in the latter, by train or bus) and a half hour commute is sort of "around the corner". By contrast, one of the factors that led to the demise of the short-lived school in Taos, New Mexico, was the general unwillingness of people in that region to expand valuable natural resources in commutes of 20 minutes or more.

(2) The size of the school population the group is aiming for in its early years

The group has to set some target for what it thinks will be a reasonable expectation for a school population in the first years of the school. Regardless of where they are located, Sudbury schools that started (or converted) in the 1990's, have all served student bodies ranging in size from 6 to 40, with most of them hovering in the range of 15-25. The fact is however that it is difficult to project into the future, because it is impossible to know when a corner will have been turned and such schools will begin attracting larger numbers from the outset. The important thing to realize here is that by focussing on a site that accommodates a certain size population, the group is also making a statement about how large a school they expect to have. Thus prospective families looking at a site that obviously is appropriate for a couple of dozen students will have to factor into their decision not only the radical educational philosophy of the school, but also the question of whether they want to become part of a school that has a small student body and only a handful of peers in any age group. On the other hand, having a sizable plant that can accommodate 100 students can be extremely discouraging to prospective families if in fact only about 2 dozen students are rattling around in its vast confines. These are not easy considerations and they don't have simple solutions. Whatever the decision, a huge element of risk is involved.

This decision is also related to the decision about where to locate. In general, a school can expect to attract a small percentage of the available target population. If there are only 50,000 people within range of the school, the anticipated size can be expected to be rather smaller than the anticipated size of a school within range of half a million people. However, no firm conclusions can be drawn on this count, because a great deal depends on factors that will be discussed in other sections, for instance the section on demographics below.

(3) The amount of money available to the group, which is connected to the decision of whether to buy or rent

A group that has no capital available to it can only hope to rent. There is no point in looking for beautiful sites that are only for sale. A good hard look at how many students the school can realistically expect to enroll in the first year (or two) will determine a budget for rent, utilities, and up-keep. That will give the group a ballpark idea of what they can spend for rent.

On the other hand, groups that do have significant capital have a lot of options, and their situation becomes much more complicated. Consider for example the following email posting agonizing over this question and asking advice from sister schools and groups.

> We are about to take the big plunge here, and I'm looking for advice before we make any giant mistakes, and throughout this scary process. We have found a beautiful 7.5 acre wooded hill plus field with a good sized stream running along two sides (with a little waterfall made of solid fossils—we found a shark's tooth in the streambed), on a quiet road just across from miles of public land. They are asking $119,000 for it, which is not too bad in this area, but, of course, a lot for us. But we can imagine this place being a forever home for the school, so with a little overconfidence and imagination, it makes sense to us to take the plunge (given our other options—zilcho).
>
> This is how we plan to do it. My husband and I are the only current founders without a mortgage or other financial strain, and the only people at this point willing to put up big bucks. (We held off on a wider fundraising drive, since we haven't had a specific goal until now; but we have reason to believe we will be able to raise a good chunk—$20-30,000—when we do make our big appeal.) We aren't able to just give the school down payment money ($40,000), but we can have it tied up for several years and forego interest on it. After consulting a real estate lawyer (our regular lawyer said it was out of his field), we think the best way to go, to make sure we don't lose our shirts if the school fails, is to buy the land ourselves, as a limited liability corporation, charge the school a rent that equals the mortgage payment under a lease-purchase agreement. The school could then buy us out as soon as it is able. The school

would come up with the building—through donations of money, skills, building materials, and volunteer labor—and be guaranteed a lease as long as it can make the mortgage payments (or even better, buy us out). If they can't, and the school folds, we would still own the land and could sell it (maybe even at a big enough profit to start the school again?).

So here are my questions: Does this arrangement make sense? If you were founders in our group would you think it was fair? I've always worried about the role of founder-financial-backer, because the power issues involved are so complex. Will I abuse my status? Will others be wary of potential abuse? Will I always feel I have to hold back my opinions because I am in danger of looking like a bully? Should we include building money in the mortgage now (and have much higher payments), or wait to see if we need it, so the pressure will be on to raise the money up front? (and risk more lawyer and banking fees and time?)

Do you think we are biting off more than we can chew? What kind of building do you recommend? (We can't do mobile classrooms.) We could go for a house-type building which would resell if the site didn't work out, or build the cheapest possible thing—a rectangular cinderblock building on slab, or do something funky like strawbale construction or dome or something. There are some fairly cheap kit houses we could put up with mostly unskilled labor. We also have access to a building supplies warehouse which donates to non-profits like us.

One exciting/frightening thought about this is that once we buy the land there will be no turning back, and a very clear path ahead of us (and sooo much work).

We have lots of people who've become part of the non-founder support group who would suddenly have to put their time and money where their mouth is. The question is, would they rise to the occasion. (I'm already getting braver about asking, now that the pressure is on.)

(4) The degree to which any given putative site conforms to the various applicable codes

This is the Achilles' heel of many a near perfect site. The more the group knows about the applicable codes, and the stronger the relationship that has been built up between the founders and the officials responsible for making decisions about whether sites conform to codes, the fewer pitfalls await. However, even with the best of preparation, last minutes glitches often arise—officials change; the same official changes his/her mind; new authorities intrude unexpectedly on the scene; codes change during the time of the search, etc. One school, convinced that it had everything in place, invested a significant sum in the purchase and in planning for the necessary improvements, only to end up abandoning the site and forfeiting their entire investment, because circumstances unfolded over time that they were not able to anticipate from the outset.

Here is the sad story of one group that ultimately failed to maintain its school, largely because of intractable site problems:

We started looking all over the county for a building. I already knew that there were hardly any places in the county that were going to be certifiable as schools, because where I have my business has to be certified, and we were trying to expand, and there just isn't any place in the county that you can just jump in and do it.

There was a town hall/community center, always just sort of hanging by a thread; not enough people used it, but it was there. Some friends suggested that we look into it. We thought we had done everything that we were supposed to, to be able to do the school there. The Town Hall managers thought it was okay. The building inspector thought it was okay. One of our founders was pretty much our building committee, and we took her at her word. So we got in there and if we're going to be generous we could say neither the Town Hall people, nor the founder, nor the building inspector knew all of the new rules, because there's new rules every year that buildings have to meet to be able to have schools in them.

It's a really nice building. Unfortunately it's a really old building, built a long, long time ago and there's no way to fix it to be able to meet school guidelines at this point. First of all you can't even get enough water, because the water main isn't big enough for the fire marshall to say you can have a school there, since you can't put in a sprinkler system. Then, there was asbestos. And it doesn't have adequate exits. It's all really lovely and you can have zillions of people in there for a Christmas fair, but oh, well.

I knew that to run a school you have to have the State fire marshall come. They have to sign off on it. So we called the fire marshall, at which point the county building inspector got into trouble for saying that we could have a school up there. That's when the building inspector got all ticked off at us. We live in a "good ole boys' society" in our county, where there are certain people who do certain things in a certain way, and if you don't talk to those State guys—if we'd never had the fire marshall come and look at it—the State would never know there was a school there.

Also we did not have the County building inspector call the State fire marshall; we called the fire marshall. We said, "We're ready for you to check us out." So we inadvertently bypassed the "good ole boys" route for getting things done, the building inspector got in trouble, and he made sure we got in trouble in a big way. He came, looked at the building, and basically closed it on the spot. We had to be out of there that day. No more school. Nobody could come the next day.

This was about a month into the school year. I think we were in denial that the Town Hall wasn't going to work out for a while, because we did try to do a bunch of the stuff they required. And it started to just build slowly: the electrical guy came and said, "Oh, these electrical things have to be done." And then there were the furnaces. Then came the big one—the issue of ingress and egress, and the narrow halls and stairs. The only way we could do it was by putting in sprinklers. There had to be a four inch main coming in to run enough sprinklers and give enough pressure. And the line on the street is only like a two inch line.

Originally, when the school closed, we had thought we would be able to go back to the town hall once we fixed all these things. We figured we'd spent ten, maybe fifteen thousand dollars fixing these things. We put in a new heater system. We tore out the massive old steamboat furnaces. We didn't know how long it was going to take us to do these things. We were doing it as quickly as we could, getting parents who knew things. People were trying to do it as well as we could without spending money we didn't have. But there was no way.

The next year, although we did become reborn in another building, in reality, when the Town Hall was lost, we lost the momentum, and were unable to bring many of the people back, even though we had a building.

Many schools open in buildings—defunct public or private schools, churches, etc.—that formerly had school permits, or similar permits, which could be grandfathered for the new school. This too has pitfalls, due to various limitations on grandfathering.

The following concise outline of procedures to follow and dangers to avoid in selecting a site was developed by a member of one group that encountered problem after problem with site after site:

I know that other schools have landed a site relatively painlessly, and that each state/county/city handles educational institutions differently, but we have assumed so many times (three or four?) that we were going to open in September '95, in January '96, in September '96.... and every time, we planned our PR around that assumption. But every time, the site we thought we had slipped through our fingers because of some regulation we had not yet discovered. I'm afraid you all might fall into the same trap we did—generating lots of enthusiasm and a big name, and then scrambling not to lose momentum as site after site faded from view and parents decided to look for other options (wondering, I think, whether we were ever going to get off the ground).

People are right in saying everything has to be done at once, but as a site-burned founder, I guess I'd always put the site first on the list. I have been intending to describe in detail to newer start-up groups what we've found out about site searches:

Step 1:

If we had known better, the first thing we would have done is make in-person appointments with the zoning person (in charge of educational institutions, if there is one) in each county and/or city in the area. (We have a city, and two counties, each with widely varying laws). At the meeting we would have copied relevant laws and/or written down each of the zoning categories in which schools are allowed. (Some differentiate between elementary and secondary schools.) Other questions to ask them: Do we need a "special exception" or variance to open a school in these zoning areas? Is there a public hearing process? Does this county/city have a law prohibiting us from sharing a building with another group (a church, women's club, Elk's Lodge, etc.)? If yes, can exceptions be made? How many acres are we required to have? How much parking? How many square feet of building space per kid? (It helps to have an imaginary school enrollment figure, like 30 kids and 6 staff.) What are the set-back requirements for buildings and parking lots? How much road frontage do we have to have? Are there any secondary or overlaid zoning categories? (Eg. in our county there are "critical areas" laws which govern the areas within 1000 feet of streams, etc., feeding into the Bay.)

Step 2:

Building Requirements.

The requirements for buildings vary somewhat but are mostly based on the BOCA code books (nationally determined building requirements, including electrical, fire safety, etc, etc) which you can read at any public library, but make little sense to lay folks like us. So you need a translator. We have a very helpful fire inspector, as well as a couple of contractor friends (use only friends, not make-a-buck big-talkers) who have helped us decipher the codes, or at least some of them. At first we wanted to find a nice old farmhouse, but that dream quickly gave way to reality... Here's the priority list for us now (this is for rentals, not buying):

1. Existing schools. Not only are they closer to the new codes, but they do not require a "change of use" permit, at least in our county, so they are not required to meet all the newest codes. That's why its easier to build a new building than to add on to the original. Adding on means the whole building has to be brought up to the latest codes.

2. Other public buildings. Offices, churches, community centers, daycares, etc. tend to be more handicap accessible, have higher capacity septic systems, and be more conducive to modification to meet codes.

3. One story buildings made of non-combustible materials. We hate cinderblock as much as anyone, but fire marshalls love it. Avoid basements and attics, which have to be sprinkled, even if you don't use them. Sprinkler systems are harder to install in pre-existing buildings (they need fatter pipes and higher water pressure). If you have public water supply, they may not be that expensive, and can get you out of some other fire code no-nos. As for stairs, they have to be enclosed with fire doors with panic bars at top and bottom, and all walls double fire-rated (that means the material in the walls has to survive a fire for two-hours instead of one). All "classrooms" have to have two exits (or sprinklers) and, upstairs, that can mean two stairways upstairs or a very elaborate fire escape. The counties seem to vary in how intensely they enforce ADA (handicap) requirements. We would have had to have handicap access to upstairs at a couple of sites we considered, so that meant ramps, which are very gradually sloped and incredibly expensive. All in all, two story buildings just seemed out of our financial range, especially if we were just renting.

Step 3:

Hire a realtor.

We tried just getting the word out to our friends and everyone else, which led to several leads, but there is no reason not to hire a commercial realtor too. It costs you nothing. The only annoying thing is having to agree to funnel leads through them so that they make the contact, not us. Our agreement is set up so that we can terminate in five days, if we want to pursue another strategy. Realtor friends have not been that helpful unless they are friends of the school too, and are really top notch realtors. The guy we are using has taught us a tremendous amount about considerations such as septic requirements for schools, possible tax benefits for landlords/sellers, requirements re access lanes off of high-use roads, and so forth. None of the half-dozen realtor friends we had knew anything about that stuff. They only dealt in residential stuff, and even that was part-time.

Share what you know about zoning and building requirements with your realtor, and with everyone else in your group. We had a little checklist we gave out at public meetings, describing what we needed in a site.

Step 4:

Find a few possible sites.

It's more efficient if you can check out several at once. Make sure the sites meet all the obvious requirements, then do the following:

1. Get the plat map of the areas and make sure you like your neighbors. Call zoning and get them to double check the sites for possible zoning problems. They might want a site plan, which at this point could be a rough sketch of the building, parking lots, road access, etc. and any changes you want to make to the site. (Ask the owners/realtor if they have one already for you to work with.)

2. Walk through the building with a builder and or fire inspector (if he/she is willing). Make a list of all the things you would need to do to bring it up to fire codes, and ADA requirements. If you can get a health inspector, they might help too. (We were very clear with ours that we would not be serving lunches. That made them relax a little.) In one place, we would have had to redo the venting system for the stove, costing us about $1000.

3. Call whatever utility companies you can to get last years heating and electric bills. One place paid $12,000/year to heat their building.

4. Make sure the owners are clear about the school's philosophy at least on a basic level (and tell them you will be carrying your own liability insurance). They also would need to know what you would have to do to get the building up to code. (That has scared most residential landlord types away from renting to us).

5. Make sure there are no neighborhood organizations which have placed restrictions on building use in their communities. Most developments around here only permit residential use. Also check the deed for restrictions on use. They can apply to renters too.

6. Bring kids and parents who are very involved in the school to the site. Kids are often very clear about what they do and don't want. It might help to schedule a short meeting afterwards, away from the realtor/owner, to talk frankly about the site. We got one realtor fuming mad by letting the kids talk us out of a site in his presence.

Step 5:

Renovation Costs

We found it necessary to get a close estimate from a contractor on whatever renovation needed to happen before we could begin negotiating a lease. I guess a building that was a real turn-key might not need this step. The cheapest renovation we encountered was around $20,000. We found it helpful to divide these costs into things which needed doing solely for school purposes and things which were generally needed (including handicap ramps on a community center, for example). That way we could argue for deductions in rent for the more general renovations.

This cost also might determine how long a lease you might ask for. The commitment level required on a so-so site might make you decide its not worth it.

We've been told that a commercial contractor is really necessary for this kind of work, but we have a very supportive residential contractor who is willing to work for almost nothing because he believes in our school. We will just have to see if our choice of commitment and cheapness over experience with commercial building is a good one.

Step 6:

Negotiation

Sadly our experience in this regard is not the greatest, since we have yet to sign a lease, or close on a purchase. But here is what we've picked up so far:

If you have a realtor who is your agent, he/she represents you in the negotiation. If they have a realtor whom you contacted directly, it is their legal responsibility to represent the other party. That means that if you tell them how high you'll go, they are required by law to let their client know that. So be careful if they have a realtor and you don't.

We were terribly afraid to be the first to propose a dollar amount for rent. I think, in retrospect, that was a mistake and made us seem devious. Our budget numbers were very tiny and made it possible for us to plead inability to pay where we felt we could get away with it. But seeming professional and viable might outweigh the usefulness of that tactic.

Being professional is really important, I think. Never showing up in hippie shorts and sandals; always being

prompt and super-organized; writing thank-you letters,
etc. are so important in this whole process, especially
with those (zoning/fire officials, etc.) whom you might
encounter again.

(5) The aesthetic ideal to which the group aspires and
against which each potential site is evaluated
It is helpful for the group to have some idea of the range
of aesthetic acceptability it is ready to pursue in a site. For
example, if the group is determined to have several acres of
land for its own use (as opposed to utilizing public lands,
for example; or having no outdoor area), then this require-
ment immediately focusses the search. It also brings into
the realm of possibility the purchase of a tract of raw land
of the size the group would like/can afford, on which a
structure can be built.

Considerations of aesthetics greatly overlap considerations of location. Thus, groups seeking to start a school
that serves an urban area might look for suburban sites in
order to have land available. Such a group also might try to
locate near urban parklands. Often, in the last analysis, the
difficulties of fulfilling all of the requirements for a site lead
groups to accept sites whose configuration is quite different
from what they had initially hoped for.

Perhaps more important than the actual features of the
site is the ambience created within whatever site the school
has ended up with. Any environment can be made pleasing
by the application of elbow grease, caring, and design, and
kept pleasing by regularly seeing to order and cleanliness.
Any space that can be transformed to feel good to the oc-
cupants is an appropriate space for a Sudbury school.

Concrete steps each group must take:

- *Promotion*

Much material on promotion is available in the Sudbury School Planning Kit, in particular the pamphlet describing the first five years of Sudbury Valley's promotional campaign, and material from other schools contained in *The 1996 Collection*. Here it might be useful to present, in brief summary form, some of the key avenues of promotion that have been utilized successfully by various groups.

Media Exposure

It is usually possible to obtain coverage in print, and on radio, for a new school in the planning stages; when it opens, television can be added to the media mix (although some schools have felt that television coverage was a little too early if they had it in their first few weeks, before the school settled in). Coverage can be obtained by directly contacting, recontacting, and hassling, various editors, reporters, and producers, who are always looking for stories to fill their space and time. As time goes by, it is harder to get this exposure, because the school is no longer "news"—one reason a school should carefully think about the timing of its television exposure. The only way to get coverage later on is to create news one way or another—hopefully not by scandal. For example, press releases can be sent out about interesting seasonal activities in the school, or about college acceptances. Any kind of new facility is also newsworthy, such as the establishment of a computer laboratory, or a music center, or a new library collection. You have to use your imagination, but often the local media are delighted to have something to present to their readers.

Radio and television talk shows are an excellent avenue for exposure through the media and actually become more readily available as the school matures and becomes better known. Sudbury schools are the kind of far-out curios that often attract producers of these shows.

Here are some examples:

> *I was lucky in that I had some connections to start with—things like the local cable television station, the local radio stations, and one local newspaper. So I called those connections and said, "Opportunity of a lifetime here. Do you want the scoop?" My energy would be very upbeat and enthusiastic: this is a scoop you don't want to miss, and brand new school, cutting edge. I would use that phrase, "cutting edge of education". I would ask for the person who covered the education stuff. "If you're the education editor, you don't want to miss this because you'd really be missing the boat on an important issue in your area". And then if they'd say, "Well, I'll think about it; I'm busy now." I'd always say, "When shall I check back with you?" I pinned them down, and I'd always follow up. I'd always check back in. I never let it go. And we did get the front page of the [major city newspaper], that was my big coup—upper right hand corner. "School has few rules" or something, some terrible headline. It was eye-catching.*

> *We saw a little article in the paper about this strange, vegetarian vendor in a local farmer's market. And they were covered by this XYZ show. I asked, "What's that?"*

They said, "It's 'Examine Your Zip Code', on public television, and they're trying to promote the diversity of [our region]. They cover things that are unique about the area". Right after I heard about that I saw in the paper that there was a new person who was going to be doing the interviewing, so we got her name. One of our students sat down and wrote a letter to the woman who was going to run the show, all about our school, saying, "It's weird, it's neat, it's fun." The letter had lots and lots of information. I didn't know what she was going to write. I just sat next to her and fielded spelling questions if she had them, but she's a very good speller. She didn't need me at all. She wrote a one page thing explaining the school, and got a call back saying, "Yeah, we want to come". We were run three times in the course of one month on public television and then they ran it again in the summer. We got a few calls and definitely recognition, definitely. That was another thing that lent credence to the school. It's on TV. It's more credible.

Informational Flyers; Catalogs

Your flyer is like your "card", and because there is a lot of information, it needs to be bigger than a business card. The sooner you begin to produce them (and they tend to change style, and to some extent content, as the school takes shape) and have them available to everyone with even a modicum of interest, the better. Even before the school has a name, and long before it has a site, it is vital to have some descriptive written materials that belong to that school group alone.

The attention and money lavished on producing a flyer is well worth the return. Well-crafted phraseology conveys a first impression of depth, intelligence and thoughtfulness. In today's world, well-crafted design and graphics are almost as important in conveying an impression of professionalism. It is not unusual to produce 500-1000 flyers on the first run, which helps keep unit costs down. Beware of producing too many thousands, because changes do happen and you want your flyers to be current; beware of producing too few, because you will be amazed at how fast they go.

Once you have these flyers, they can be distributed in myriad ways: they can be handed to friends to hand to friends; they can *and should* be stocked in every public library in the area, and in many stores and professional offices; they can be used in bulk mailings; they can serve as the key item in responses to inquiries, in addition to any cover letter that might be used; they can be used as introductory pieces for professional educators and media personnel; and they can be given to family and friends when they start asking, "So, what are you doing these days?"

Unfortunately, only a few schools have created catalogs, which are much more elaborate than flyers, with even more information. School catalogs describe the essential features of the educational foundations of the school, portray something of the life and spirit of the school, and outline the way the school functions as a community. A comprehensive catalog conveys to others how seriously you take the enterprise and how seriously you wish them to take it. Catalogs can be prepared as soon as a realistic target date has been set for the opening of the school. Catalogs are expensive to produce, but a person receiving one comes away with the impression that they are dealing with a solid institution, based on a substantial foundation of experience and theory.

Remember, for a long time the flyers and catalogs serve as the only thing identifying you that people can actually experience.

Informational Meetings

One way to attract community interest has been used by virtually every startup group—namely, public meetings set up for the declared purpose of conveying information about the new school being proposed. These meetings can be held at homes, public meeting places (secular or religious), cafes, or at the school site itself, if it exists. It is important to spread the word as widely as possible about such meetings, as it is very hard at any time of the year to get much of a crowd for such occasions. Usually, posters are made and placed in libraries, stores, public buildings, bulletin boards, and on lamp-posts if possible; people are asked to tell their friends and acquaintances; and flyers are mailed to whatever mailing lists(s) are available and deemed useful.

Here are several accounts of experiences with meetings of this sort:

> *In December we sent out a letter with a school proposal, and announced four public meeting dates. It was very important to practice talking about it with our families. One day we were sitting around after dinner, and I said, "Would it be ok if we talked about this school we want to start?" It was a friendly room, but they challenged us. So that was a real good scrimmage, if you will. And then we did the same thing with*

another family, which was less friendly from the outset. We did that at Thanksgiving.

*The meetings were held at the public library. We did the same thing each time. We had apple juice and cookies or something like that. We presented our idea and then we introduced ourselves; it was mostly question and answer. We also spliced together some things from Sudbury Valley onto one video, a ten minute thing, and showed that as well. And we started selling Sudbury Valley materials which was enormously helpful. We gave away **And Now for Something Completely Different**, and something called a New School Fact Sheet. After one of those meetings another founding member joined us who has been very helpful. That was kind of a turning point because she's a go-getter, would keep us on our toes a lot. It was wonderful to have found her through that public meeting.*

I gave a public meeting, realizing that maybe it isn't good to limit this to a circle of friends. Instead, let's see who in the community is interested. So we got a public space. I made up flyers, I got them around town for a couple of weeks, posted them, talked to people, handed them out. Told all my friends, "Can you pass it on to somebody else that might be interested?". That was in a municipal hall, which cost $40. I wrote a twelve page speech. I thought maybe I wasn't giving enough background information, or didn't have my thoughts together completely, so I wanted to avoid the mistake of not having myself be clear.

So I sat there and read for a bit. It was fifteen minutes of me explaining things. To some people, that was tortuously long, but to other people it wasn't. One person, I found out later, was really moved; he is a twelve year old boy, and he sat and listened to every word. He didn't go through a long discussion with me, but he heard people say, "Don't talk so much next time." He said, "Well, what do you mean? You know for me that really meant something?" Then he realized that everybody doesn't feel that way, but for him it really worked. I realized okay, it has to be somewhere in the middle.

At the second meeting maybe thirty people attended. There were some people who just stood up and left. That really bummed me out. There was a sixteen year old boy that came. I had talked to him before. He was standing by the door. His mother knew about Sudbury Valley and said it would probably be a good idea if he came and heard about our school. But his father came and not his mother. Literally, during my speech, the father stood up, yanked his son by the arm, and got the hell out of there. That was the last I saw of him.

So we have some founders' meetings and decide to go public again, to try a different thing. Not spend any money, have a friendlier atmosphere, maybe. There's a coffeehouse here in town where you can get some free time. If any social injustice is being addressed, you can come speak. So I got four nights there, two week nights and two weekend nights—four weeks in a row. Those got in the paper, to make sure people knew what the times were. At that point, we started to generate a group of people.

I was never, ever, a public speaker. That changed during this time. Before the first time I gave a speech I was really concerned about it. And then a group of people started to happen. Some people would show up who really had questions, and I tried to give them the best response I could, and I realized I didn't have time to worry about giving a speech—that didn't enter into it any more.

One of our founders started off with private viewings in her home of the **Introduction to Sudbury Valley School** *video which people discussed after watching it together. This has worked for us until the present. We changed the name to Philosophy Discussions for a while and held them in different community buildings around the metropolitan area. Sometimes we even had specialized topics like Freedom to Learn, The Judicial System of our school, Daily Life at our school, Talking with Students and Staff of our school, etc. These meetings were advertised by word of mouth, informational tables at fairs and stores, community calendars in local papers, and mailings to school counselors, principals, and preschool directors.*

The mailing list is continually being added to each time we have a public event. The meetings now are known to our community as Talkabouts. We have scheduled seven this year, from February to August. In our short history, we have noticed a pattern of increased enrollment from January to May. Thus we begin the Talkabouts early in the year and continue until school begins.

The value of informational meetings does not necessarily end with the opening of the school. Most schools continue to schedule them as part of a continuing program to attract interest in the broader community. They are also often useful for members of the school community, especially new parents, as a means of furthering their understanding of the school's philosophy and practice.

Public Events

A different way to win public notice is to stage large-scale events which have some degree of mass appeal. These almost always have to feature some fairly well-known guest, or at least a credentialed guest from another part of the country! Events of this sort can usually attract fair-sized audiences, at least by comparison with the informational meetings.

To make such meetings a success can take no small amount of money. Usually, a fair-sized, fairly well-known hall has to be rented. The cost of advertising and mailing can add up, because the more resources the group puts into advertising the event, the more likely it is that a good turnout can be expected. Refreshments are a good idea, but not absolutely necessary. And then there are the expenses for the speaker, travel expenses, if necessary, and perhaps a fee. On the other hand, big events of this sort generate a lot of free publicity, since the media often are willing to cover them, and they can be listed among all sorts of community announcements on radio, tv and in daily and weekly newspapers. Often a guest speaker from afar generates media interest as a personality in addition to the coverage of the event.

A Sudbury Valley alumnus can be an attraction, whether or not they are well-known. Here's what happened with one:

In March we produced our first Newsletter. A friend of ours put that together for free and it was really nice.

In it, we announced our meeting with a local Sudbury Valley alumnus. Lots of people came to that meeting and had lots of questions. We advertised the meeting through our maillist, and with a lot of postings of flyers in libraries and supermarkets and places like that. We also were in a small local paper which is distributed fairly widely. It's a local weekly and it worked out really well for us. Free advertising, listings in their calendar, a couple of articles.

The alum was tremendous. He just sat up in front and we did our little introductions and then we said, "Oh, this is someone who went to Sudbury Valley School for twelve years." And then we trotted out his resume and jaws dropped. He said great things. At one point, there were some relatively confrontational people in the crowd. He said, "Look, do you trust these people who are founding the school? That's what you have to decide. Do these seem like reasonable, nice people? If you think so, then the school will work." It was a really good meeting.

In planning an event of this sort, there is a danger that has to be taken into account. Sometimes groups look for speakers whose names are well-known, and whose views seem at first glance to correspond to the underlying philosophy of the school. *Most of the time, on closer reading, it turns out that there are crucial differences between the putative speaker's views and those the founders are trying to promote.* Also, such speakers tend to bring out audiences that are sympathetic to their outlook, and the result can be that both the speaker and most of the audience will be focussing on something at best irrelevant to, and at worst opposed to, the founding of a Sudbury school.

Open Houses

These are occasions for the general public to meet and speak informally with staff, students, and parents in an ongoing (or just about to open) school. They are best held on site, since people who attend them want, among other things, to see what the plant looks like. Occasionally a small talk can be scheduled as part of the event.

Open houses are of limited value. First and foremost, there are only so many times that the students in the school wish to be "goldfish in a bowl". Second, the students present at an open house are not always to be depended on to display their best behaviors—in fact, students in school while their parents are visiting often do not behave terribly well, and this can have a powerfully unpleasant affect on strangers. Then, there is only so much that can be seen or conveyed about the day to day life of the school in such a setting, and it is especially easy to generate wild mis-impressions of the school. This is especially unfortunate when visitors try to use an open house in lieu of an admissions interview, because it is easy and free.

Not every group to date has used open houses, and not all who have are pleased with them as a recruitment or public relations vehicle. They take a lot of work and they do not seem as productive as some of the other avenues. On the other hand, an open house that generates one new enrollment (that would not have come anyway) is by definition very successful.

Mass Mailings

By these we do not mean mailings to your own carefully and painstakingly generated mailing list, but rather mailings to sub-sets of the general population that seem likely to be interested in your message. For instance, mass mailings can (and usually should) be made to certain kinds of educational professionals in your area—specifically, school guidance counselors, school psychologists, educational consultants, and school principals. These people should be made acquainted with your plans for starting a specific new kind of school in their area, and should be consistently reminded of your existence from time to time.

Various subscriber mailing lists are available from periodicals whose readers may be interested in the school. One such proven journal is *Mothering Magazine*; other titles might include those of environmental magazines, local parenting papers, natural living journals, new age and holistic papers and journals, and parenting magazines. Sometimes one might consider using broader lists—for instance, at Sudbury Valley we once mailed (with disappointing results at the time that this was done) to all local parents of kids ages 6-12.

Usually there are minimum numbers of address labels that can be ordered, and often the minimum is larger than you can use, because it may cover a much wider area than you are interested in. But the labels are cheap: the expensive part is the piece of mail itself, which should be polished and professional in order to compete with the barrels of junk mail every household receives. The post office issues bulk permits to non-profit organizations that allow you to make bulk mailings at a very low postal rate, but the permits themselves are expensive, and are only worth it if you plan several bulk mailings or a humongous one.

The mass mailing industry considers a 1-2% return on mass mailings to be a success, so that is a figure that you can factor in when considering whether you want to pursue this avenue, or whether your pursuit has been successful, at least by industry standards.

Speaking Engagements

One avenue of promotion that Sudbury Valley has pursued pretty consistently from the beginning is soliciting opportunities to speak before community groups of one kind or another. These include such varied groups as PTO's (mostly associated with elementary schools), religious organizations (including church services, e.g., in Unitarian Universalist Churches), professional groups within the educational establishment (such as school counselors' or teachers' organizations), fraternal organizations such as Rotary Clubs, and other civic and private social groups. Also, opportunities to speak before classes in education at local colleges and universities have been vigorously sought. By looking for such opportunities year after year, the school's message has slowly been broadcast in the general community, giving the school more currency, exposure, and legitimacy.

Carrying out such a program requires a lot of time and energy. To date, as far as we know, few if any new schools and start up groups have set this activity high enough on their list of priorities to allocate substantial resources to it. Therefore we have no indication of the extent to which these activities, if they were vigorously pursued, would be useful in enhancing a school's success.

Fairs, Conferences, etc.

Different regions of the country offer different kinds of opportunities for publicity. For example, in one city, a unique operation offered an opportunity to man a table and make a presentation:

> *Club of Choices has been going on since '89. It's a forum for alternative thinkers. One couple was Swedish and they feel that they have communicated with all the twelve disciples from all twelve different universes. I leave my mind very open and just treat it like a smorgasbord, taking what I want and leaving what I don't.*
>
> *The basic idea is to open your mind to all possibilities of life. That the path is absolutely open. They have networking tables where people sell their wares—like a little gypsy caravan kind of thing. Then you go in and you have a vegetarian dinner, and then there are speakers. There's like an opener and then there's the big show, the headliner.*

Another group took advantage of a special kind of annual fair held in its area:

> *We had a table at the Common Ground Fair. We had two and a half pages of sign-ups at the fair; that was the best advertising venue we have ever had. Common Ground Fair is an organic farmers' and gardeners' association and it's an institution in this state. It's about ten years old, maybe a little older. The Common Ground Fair is the back to the land, hippies, alternative lifestyles group and it's huge now. It's been huge for a long time. And everybody who is not back to the land hippies dresses up like a back to the land hippy for the day.*
>
> *They have all sorts of organic food and there's no sugar and there's no coffee and it's very pure. So there are coffee stands outside in the parking lot: "Last chance*

for coffee." The catch was that, in order to have a table, you have to sign up nine months ahead of time. We had never done it just because we had never gotten collected enough to do it ahead of time. This year we did it and we were there for three days, and Waldorf was there, maybe a Montessori school was there. They've always been there. We were not put near each other for some reason. We were in a tent near the Green Party and a bookstore was the next booth. It was incredible. Hundreds of people came by and didn't do anything. We had all the Sudbury Valley things and sold nothing, but we sold a couple of our T-shirts and we gave away a lot of flyers, a lot of bookmarks, and a lot of people signed up. We've had a number of interviews.

Many groups are convinced that it is helpful to make themselves known within local homeschooling organizations, especially as the number of homeschoolers (particularly "unschoolers") continues to grow rapidly.

We went to a homeschooling conference in April. We had our little rinky dink setup. People had these elaborate little booths and so forth, and they were selling their books and all their materials for the homeschoolers. We had a card table and a handwritten sign. We had no idea that people would be this fancy. But we had the Sudbury Valley books all displayed as nicely as we could possibly get them and then our Newsletters. We were swamped with people. There were a million people signing up on our mailing list and buying books and it was a great thing, I think. We actually did attract three families from that conference who are very interested. So that turned out to be a very good thing that we did, even though we like to shy away from homeschoolers. It worked out.

The point is, it wasn't only the religion-oriented homeschooling people. It included the hard-to-find homeschooling crowd, the invisible homeschoolers who are hard to get hold of, so it was cool.

Some of the problems associated with appealing to homeschoolers will be discussed further on. Unfortunately there do not seem to be many other forums aimed at people looking for alternative schools, although occasionally one comes across events for schools of all types, or conferences aimed at parents. Keeping your eyes open for opportunities to be at places where parents are targeted is a good plan. Here is what one group had to say:

*We advertise with homeschooling conferences. We always send them something to go in their information bag. We used to have a booth, but that got too expensive, and it wasn't worth that much money. On the other hand, we don't think education fairs are the place for us. They're really expensive, and I still don't see us in a huge hall like that with a lot of other schools. We did the **Mothering Magazine** support network, a group that has a lot of like-minded people, and I think we're going to pursue that more.*

Many communities have support groups specifically designed for readers of ***Mothering Magazine***, and these would seem to be fruitful avenues to pursue. Similarly, many communities have La Leche League conferences or forums on parenting where a table can be rented, and sometimes a presentation can even be arranged.

The mainstream education group most likely to pay attention to the founding of a Sudbury school is the state or local school counselors' association. Counselors are usually the first people approached by students and parents whose ideas are not in harmony with those of the school they attend. Getting exposure in a state-wide or regional counselors' association conference is thus more likely than other venues to attract the attention of people who might eventually make referrals to your school.

Sale of Books, etc., about the Model

There is a wealth of material published by the Sudbury Valley School Press about the Sudbury model. The Planning Kit contains copies of almost all of the available materials, as well as the details of the consignment program, offered by the Press to all purchasers of Planning Kits. Consignment offers all startup groups a method of stocking Press materials at no cost to the group, and selling them at a small profit to the group.

These materials are extremely helpful in providing useful background and in-depth exploration of the fundamental ideas upon which the model is based to prospective founders, staff members, parents, students, and media representatives. Groups that take advantage of these materials have at their disposal the product of several decades of experience and thought related to the development of the model. Of course there is particular value to literature and other materials developed within a group's own membership, since this enriches and deepens the group's understanding of the model in addition to increasing the public's confidence in the group's ability to articulate its goals.

Advertising

One of the most difficult decisions to make is whether to spend the comparatively large sums of money involved in media advertising. Some groups, including Sudbury Valley School, have found that all forms of advertising available to schools on a relatively modest budget are virtually useless in producing enrollment inquiries, or other identifiable substantive responses. On the other hand, some groups consider that ads have been useful, due to the special nature of the vehicle in which the advertising appears. Here is what one group said:

> *The newspaper, which is on the left, and has a state-wide circulation, was very helpful because it got people thinking about us. They told their friends and we got a kid out of it and we got a staff member out of it. That newspaper folded, but the people who were working on it have now started a new one, and we're advertising in that. So I think that newspapers that target our kind of people work and the others don't.*

Another group put much more of their resources into advertising:

> *The two area parents' papers have been our expensive advertising. They're both tabloids. They hit mostly yuppies with younger kids. The typical person reading that has a preschooler or early elementary age child.*
>
> *We spent over $4,000 on ads in these two parent magazine tabloids. And we only got one kid as a result of that advertising. We will get his siblings, and the parents love the school.*

We have learned some things about PR. We know now that there are some times when advertising is very effective at getting a lot of people in here to hear our story. Basically it's the February, March period. If you have the budget, January and April would be useful additions, particularly January. February and March ads will fill this place up with people who are interested in hearing about us, people who have read enough in the ad to know a little bit of what we're about. Not a wholly inappropriate group of people. So we'll do the quarter page ads. They cost like $400-$500 per issue. We'll probably have 200 inquiries that result from those ads.

We talk to each person on the phone. It depends on who answers the phone as to what kind of treatment they get. The staff members are better than the kids at dealing with this kind of inquiry. And staff members vary, based on their personalities, as to how they handle them. My personal approach is that I take their name and address and where they heard about the school, and I tell them a little bit about the school. Just three sentences. I try to hold it to just a few sentences, telling them it's a place where kids control their own time and activities. And I try to get them to tell me what they're looking for, so that they can, after they hear what this school is about in a few sentences, try to tell me why they're looking for the kind of school that I've just told them we are. That's a natural human tendency to want to communicate with somebody. After all, they called us for a reason, so they know a little bit about us. I also say we have informational meetings once a month, and ask if they have any other questions. Usually they don't ask any other questions, and they just want to read the stuff. But a third of the time they have some question or two. Or they want to tell you about their particular situation to see if there's a fit. It's very hard to listen. It's much easier just to talk and talk and talk about what the school's about. I used to do that. Sometimes I still do it.

The same group also appeared in a local educational directory published by a newspaper in which it was advertising. The listing turned out to get a better response than the ads:

We didn't write our entry. Somebody else wrote it for us. I didn't know you were supposed to provide the thing written. They called up, I talked to them. They called up because we were advertising there, and from reading our stuff, they just said, "no curriculum." When I saw it I kind of cringed, because you can put it more nicely. However that word was more effective than all the advertising we ever did, combined. We got more kids and more staff, and everything from "no curriculum" in that parents' paper than we ever did from all the ads we ever did.

Here's how one of the people attracted by the listing responded:

One of the regional information newspapers for parents ran their annual private school directory that listed everything, from whether they had uniforms to almost anything else. I was just scanning through there. I was homeschooling at the time and not even looking for a school, but I was captive somewhere and that was the only reading material. Scanning down I saw something that said, "no curriculum" and called. All the other schools listed said things like, "child-centered curriculum with focus on developing children's unique whatever"; "heavy emphasis on phonics"; stuff like that.

As far as we know, no one has had the ability to advertise on television, and only Sudbury Valley has advertised on radio, and that hardly at all. These ads are extremely expensive and are not usually considered to be an effective promotional medium unless they can be repeated with some degree of frequency and consistency.

Whatever the promotional mechanism used, the most important fact to remember is that what counts most is multiple exposure, not the impact of a single media appearance, no matter how flashy that appearance is, nor how well it comes across. One front page news article, one evening news tv segment, one radio talk show, one well-attended public event, one bulk mailing, a table at one fair—one anything, alone, has at best a fleeting impact. What you want is to have people encounter your name as often as possible, and in as many different contexts as possible. As one person put it:

With all the PR stuff, our name is getting out there so much that people know that we're not an elementary school or a preschool anymore. The whole advertisement thing—you have to go how many times, twenty-seven times, before they'll know your real name? Some outrageous number, before people recognize your name in the area. It's amazing.

As time passes—and it takes time; make no mistake about that—and as the promotional effort is steadfastly pursued, the school's name will enter into the consciousness of an ever-increasing number of people in your area. The fact that your school's name keeps appearing and reappearing will give the school some credibility in and of itself, a credibility that will be reinforced by a track record of continuing successful operation year after year.

Demographics

There is no indication at all as to what sort of demographics favors a successful Sudbury school. This type of school, at this point in history, appeals to only a tiny percentage of the population anywhere, and not necessarily the same percentage everywhere. Thus, even a lightly populated area, if it has the right constellation of world views represented among its families, can sustain such a school, while it is sometimes almost impossible to get one going in a large metropolitan area which exhibits hostility towards treating children as responsible beings.

To give some idea of the demographic diversity we are talking about, here are some descriptions given by members of existing schools:

Median income in this area is $28,600; median home value is $80,000. There is low unemployment. There is a split in the community between the local blue collar workers and the educated managerial class that are frequently "from away"—upper middle class people who work in the state capital, seven miles away. This is the bedroom community for them, partly. I would say maybe ten percent of the community is that. So it's basically a blue collar area and rural. There's a certain number that are artsy-craftsy, back-to-the-land types around. We have gotten very few of those, and I don't know why. They've been in touch with us.

This town's population is about seven thousand. But we have quite a large area that we draw from; people within about a thirty-five minute drive.

We feel that the demographics of the area is a limiting factor. It's a very low population density, and our kids are drawn almost exclusively from middle class and upper middle class families. We wish it wasn't like that, obviously. But it is at this point. I don't think we have any working class families. There's no tradition of alternative education. We are the only alternative school in this area. There never has been one. There are Christian schools around, but not even many of those.

This is a university area. The state university is its major industry. I'd say it's a very mixed area. On the one hand there is a very large academic audience. On the other hand there's a very large working class audience. In the last fifteen years a lot of professional people have moved in who are not associated with the university. We're also thirty minutes from a large city, so you get a lot of commuters. And there is a certain rural component to the community. The town the school is actually in is all rural with a population of 1,400; it's a dairy town.

University people were extremely unresponsive. For instance, when we had a conference, we sent out over a thousand brochures, but not one person from the university came to the conference. The conference was held in the local high school of the university town. One faculty person from the high school came to the conference! I was absolutely as cynical and disgusted as I could be. I wasn't so cynical in the beginning. I was more naive. For instance we thought maybe the education department would be interested in us being some kind of a lab school or something like that, but they didn't want to touch us with a ten foot pole. I think that professional people tend to be afraid of us, too. I would say that the people who are more willing to take the risks to be here are kind of down to earth, more grounded people. They don't live in their heads so much. I would say the more intellectual a person is, the more likely they are to be threatened by us, probably because they're more invested in living a particular lifestyle and wanting their kids to follow suit and believing that the way to do that is to follow a particular track.

A lot of people in this area come to live here for the way of life, and the weather; many times these are people who prefer not to work, and chose to live simply rather than have to spend a lot of hours at a job. Normal winter weather is 65 degrees. It doesn't get cold. So there is really a whole consciousness to this area, and we are not able to charge the tuition that another Sudbury school is charging just an hour or so away. We could never charge that much money. A lot of people commute to the computer industry, but we have a huge number of artists—it's a real artists' community. People have creative, alternative ways of making a living. One of our staff, for instance, has a bicycle delivery business.

As a friend said when he came to visit, "No wonder you have no kids in your school; nobody lives up here." Our population is under 3,000. A city with 30,000 people and 50,000 in the metropolitan area is about 45 minutes from here. I think our town is considered to be out in the boondocks. There's very little traffic from the city down this way. We've done a lot of advertising and PR work there and sometimes we'll get educators that call us, but never parents.

This town is situated where it's on the way to nowhere, really. So people don't come here. The closest town has 5,000 and there's nothing else really around here besides those two towns that's close enough to draw from.

On the other hand, when we moved here a bunch of the houses were just kind of decrepit places, and a lot of younger people have since moved in with kids. It's got a revitalized feeling of being a nice, small town; a really stereotypical New England town, with porches and curving streets. That's why we moved here, all of us. It's a quiet, safe, little town, sort of out of the way.

But there is a certain problem of flatlanders versus old-timers. At town meetings people will express some resentment toward the people like us who have moved in who haven't necessarily grown up in this state. So, sometimes, there's division. None of the families in our school are old-timers.

*It's a real struggle for some of our families to pay tuition. We have people who do computer graphics; a musician; a carpenter; the owner of a print shop; a psychotherapist; a farmer, a baker, and someone who works at the bakery. I think **most** of the people in the school now have to work hard at paying tuition. There have been a couple of families where it hasn't been a struggle, but they've all left. I wonder what that says.*

Our area has about a million and a half people. The biggest employer used to be military, but one base has been shut down, and they're shutting down the other.

This city is the capital of the state. We have the best highways in the whole state! The state hasn't particularly been friendly to business, so a lot of it has left. But there still are quite a few industrial jobs. It's coming on strong toward being a base for higher technology—we're becoming a new silicon valley in a way.

Basically it's a middle income area. I would say that the people who come to our school are in a very moderate level.

Twenty percent of the population in this county is Asian, 20% Hispanic, 3% black, 57% white. This county had a tiny population just fifty years ago. It was all agricultural land. And it boomed after World War II. But they've had limits on development, consistently, so it's expensive to live here, and expensive to buy a home. It would be difficult for a poor person to move here, or even a middle income person. Because median home price is two hundred and some thousand dollars. Your average, working class American family would have trouble moving here.

It's unbelievable, driving around here, the number of high tech firms. All the way from the very biggest to countless little companies.

This town has 50,000; the whole area we are in has several million.

Our area is the fortieth largest market nationally. But it is considered economically very conservative; national marketers do not introduce new products in this area, and will never use this as a test market. This is one of the later markets to be developed because it's resistant to new products, and so it doesn't provide a good test of how a product is going to fly nationally.

Politically, the region is, by registration, about two to one Republican to Democrats. There are Democratic concentrations within the city limits, but in some of the outlying areas, the registration difference is even more dramatic. In some municipalities and in some townships it's four to one Republican to Democrats. Independents don't get to vote in primaries here, so the independent registrations are fairly minor.

One of the demographic factors that we've noticed is a high proportion of families who have self-employeds. Where nationally the number is about one in six, at one point we had something like three-fourths of families who were relying on self-employment income. Of course that knocked us for a loop in the recession, because self-employeds usually take a recession worse than others.

There's a lot of federal employment here. There are two major military supply depots. State government is a major employer and the distribution industry is extremely heavy in this area—trucking, the train yards.

An aspect where I see a difference compared to the standard for the area is religious affiliation. This community is largely WASP and the composition of the school community is not highly Christian. We've had a lot of religious diversity over the years.

These are the two things that stand out most to me: the entrepreneurial streak and the religious diversity.

Here, for the purposes of comparison, are demographics for schools that managed to open but found it impossible to remain in operation.

This city has about three and a half million people. It's an enormous metropolitan area. We are focussing on the area west of Center City, which has about half a million people. This isn't young, lower middle income families; this is 35 year-old professional singles, or married without children, and small older families with children. This is the most expensive corridor, probably, to live in, mostly white collar professionals.

The local public school district is the worst school district in this general area. People go to private schools. There's a little elitism going on.

We focused where the avant garde, the real alternative people, live here. I think real estate will be a little more affordable out here and we won't have the same code restrictions.

This is a very small community. However, I had been living here for 24 years, so I knew everybody. I just sort of knew where people were at. If they were dissatisfied at all, if they'd ever complained to me about education at all, they got a phone call.

In the whole county, there are 175,000 people, maybe. That's everybody, including the students at the state university, the people from the army base, and all the state workers because we are the capital city. There aren't many people who make big money; everybody pretty much goes to public school. There are little, teeny religious schools, and there are homeschoolers. Nobody knows how many homeschoolers there are, because you don't have to register until you're eight years old in this state. And there are survivalists. There was a group of them that were interested in this, but because of their survivalist tendencies, they're not making any money, and none of them had any money. I would get harassing phone calls when I would say we were going to charge money, because there are a lot of alternative people around, and many believe that you should have sliding fee scales, and that if you're really alternative you should be rewarded, and therefore not pay any money. I would get mean phone calls, saying, "Well how do you expect me to go if you're going to charge money?" I would say, "Well, how do you expect us to do it if we don't charge money?"

In and of itself, there is little in the demographics of these three schools that would seem to predict their failure, which must therefore be due to other factors. Similarly, there is nothing in the demographics *per se* of the following group to indicate why it has been unable to get a school going yet despite several years of effort:

Country folk used to live here. I went to school with kids who didn't go to school the first two weeks because they were out picking tobacco and they had to do it because they needed to put food on the table. In the last ten or fifteen years, it's changed a lot. A lot of people from the city are moving here so it's become a richer county. People commute into the city and sometimes they take their kids with them and put them in schools there because there's not much of an option here. It's becoming a bedroom community, with three major cities less than an hour away.

There are a lot of government workers. There are still some farmers, but not nearly as many as there used to be. The general trend is farms being sold and subdivided.

All in all it is simply too early in the history of Sudbury schools, and there are too few such schools, for a meaningful market analysis to be made that would identify communities which show a particular inclination toward accepting such schools.

Staffing a Sudbury School

There comes a point in the founding process of every school when the leap has to be taken into concretizing the first year's staff. To understand the nature of this leap, we have to describe the natural history of a Sudbury-model staff. Let's start by looking at the two end points.

All schools begin with a set of ur-founders. All schools that succeed in opening and remaining in operation, end up with a staff that is chosen by the school community. In every case there is a significant overlap between the ur-founder group and the people who become the staff when the school opens. How and why does this come about?

Whatever initial motivation brought the ur-founders to the notion of starting a school, by definition they are all people who have decided that they want to become deeply and actively involved in the successful establishment of a Sudbury school. This means that they already have the mindset that they will do whatever is necessary to get a school up and running, at least through its opening phases. This fact suggests that the ur-founders are more than likely to be ready, if not always eager, to take on the duties of the initial staff. At the time that ur-founders make the commitment to becoming founders, they may not all have the idea of becoming staff; but this idea must begin to permeate their consciousness as they realize the exact nature of the task ahead.

As the founding group gets formed, more people become involved for a variety of motives, one of which may be
to eventually become a staff member in a Sudbury school.
With each passing month, two parallel processes inevitably
unfold: one, the consolidation (with all the attendant strife
and division that this process may entail) of a group of
founders who are focussed on the same concept of a school;
and two, the gradual emergence of a sub-group that sees
itself as the initial staff. The problem every school faces,
in one form or another, is to create a procedure whereby
the actual staff gets chosen in a manner that takes into
account both the emerging self-selected group of hopeful
staff members and the realistic staff needs of the school as
perceived by the founding group as a whole. Creating such
a procedure is complicated by an inexorable truth that every
group has to face: that whatever the procedure is, it cannot
be the same as, or even much similar to, the end point of
community chosen staff that is the goal of every school.
This is because the concept of community takes a radical
jump when the school actually opens—namely, from that
of a group of founders (the nature of whose involvement
with the soon to be founded school is as yet unknown) to
that of a community of students, parents and staff, trustees
and public members who are actually involved, one way or
another, in the operation of an existing institution.

So, in reality, here is what actually happens. Somehow,
either by consensus or after some intense processing,
the founders get a fairly good idea of who they want the
initial staff to be. Sometimes, that is all that happens
and the school opens with that slightly amorphous group
as staff, leaving them to work out the formalities among
themselves. Other times the founders struggle to create

a formal procedure that will validate their choices, and that occasionally also leads to the incorporation of some wholly new person. Probably the most important thing to remember is that there is absolutely no way for anybody to know in advance of the school's beginning operating how any particular person will perform as a staff member, even if the person has been a student or a staff member at another Sudbury school. Until the actual interactions between the members of a living community building its culture begin to transpire, no one can be sure that any particular person will be comfortable as a staff member or that the community will be comfortable with him/her.

Here are a few samples of the way initial staff was chosen in some schools:

Initially the founders were worried about finding staff. The Staff Selection Committee publicized and held a meeting that drew about 35 people, at which point it was very clear there were more people who would apply for this job than there were jobs, and we let go of that concern. We said very clearly at that meeting, and then subsequently behaved in a way that actually proved that we meant it, that you couldn't apply for this job; you had to work your way into this job. That we were going to do the best we could, but the only way we could measure people was by the work they had done towards getting the school up and running, not by their professional data, or any other way. Of course a number of people dropped out as soon as that was the news. But other people started working on committees to make the school happen. So in that sense it was quite a successful meeting. But the main way it was a successful meeting is that it took community anxiety and absolutely moved it on.

The main players didn't do a lot of sorting out and, as it turned out, different people had different visions of what the school really was. I think we took a lot on faith and we trusted the people who were able to deliver— able to go to meetings, take on responsibility, deliver the goods. However, there was competition from the very beginning. The Staff Selection Committee came up with hiring criteria. The Business Meeting [the formal founding group] set the staff budget and they set the full-time equivalents.

I'd like to think that in the staff election process that all issues, substantive and personal, are talked about: people's strengths and weaknesses, or benefits to the school. None of that happened at our first staff election, before the school started, with the Business Meeting. Each person spoke for two minutes. No questions.

This is how the staff developed. In the beginning, in my mind, I always knew that H. would be staff. I had no problems with him personally. I had no reason that I didn't want him to be staff, and I knew that he wanted to do that and I had trust in his commitment and dedication. We wanted two people.

Then there was the fiasco of the staff interviews. K. was interviewed, but was too poor to not get paid for that long. The Board decided the democratic thing to do would be that whoever wanted to be a staff person could write a letter of intent to the Board and submit to an interview process. And then there would be some decision.

One family wanted that. We all knew each other. We didn't have to go through interviews. The people who wanted the interviews were people who didn't like and didn't trust what the obvious momentum was. That family had someone in mind they wanted on staff—a Montessori teacher, someone with a lot of vim, who was going to bring a lot of interesting things for the kids to do. So from their point of view this interview process was to weed out people that we had already kind of assumed were going to be on staff.

It wasn't really an interview about staff. It was about people who were on the Board being able to do something that they needed to do. Some process that they needed to do. So the rest of us went along with it. But the person they wanted to participate in it didn't play. I think that family then officially withdrew.

So we had the whole summer to go, and we hadn't really settled the staff; we just knew that H. was going to be on staff. Then B. volunteered. I remember the meeting where she said, "I am willing to give a year of my time as volunteer staff." And we were all very grateful to her. So we knew we had H. and B., and that was settled.

Mostly our founding group was parents, not people who wanted to be on staff. We wanted a school for our kids. We didn't think we were going to be staffing it. I talked with other schools a lot about staff, and what makes a good staff member. We were quite troubled about it.

For staff, we were looking for people who were known to be good with kids. The founders didn't really consider themselves to be in that category, so we were looking elsewhere. We didn't have a School Meeting yet to elect the staff, so we tried to set up an election procedure that would be as much like it as we could. We created a questionnaire that prospective staff can answer, and we arranged for the prospective staff, the people who showed up, to get to meet the kids who were at that time enrolled in the non-existent school.

The questionnaire was really helpful. There were trick questions, really, to kind of lead people down the wrong path. In most of the cases the proper answer was "nothing". "What do you do when . . . ?" People would say, "Oh, well, I would . . .", and they'd spout these beautiful techniques that they have for working with kids.

We had one applicant, whom we all liked. She was a wonderful young woman, and the kids loved her and we all loved her. We didn't know her that well, but we all just liked her. She's one of these people that you just like to be around. She didn't quite satisfy the requirements that we had set up to make people eligible for the election in the time frame that she was supposed to do it. We set up these hurdles, these hoops you had to jump through, and she just didn't quite manage to jump through all of them. They had to study the model, they had to answer this questionnaire, they had to join the founding group, which meant coming to founders' meetings, paying all the founders' dues. They had to become founders in order to run for staff. She didn't want to pay the back dues. She was poor, so we just let it slide. We put her on the ballot anyway.

I think it was the first real "nitty-gritty, go into the whole mode and see what it is". We learned something really important, that keeps coming up. It's that you set up certain guidelines and you have to follow them. You set up the guidelines for a reason. You need to have flexibility, especially when you're new, but you can't just say, "Well, this didn't work, let's throw it away". You can't just blow it off. Even in small ways, it comes back to get you. And that's what happened in that election. We kind of flexed the requirements a little bit, because we weren't "inflexible". And this one person overwhelmingly won the staff election. Way more votes than anybody else. And then she disappeared. Nobody really knew her. We just liked her, and we didn't really know what we wanted in a staff person, and I think that because we liked her so much we kind of got this idea, that this is the magic staff person that's going to be what we need. It was really weird, it was like a group hallucination.

Part of the staff thing was it's no mystery who should be on staff. We were making it look like we had to find some staff, or that we didn't know who they were, or we didn't know who they should be or what they should be. But really it was like we should look closer to home. Look where you are.

Our staff, the first year, were mostly parents. For one thing, we had to work for free the first year. How many people are willing to do that? Well, the most devoted, and those are the ones who should be there anyway, because they're people who really care enough about the philosophy, and making this kind of environment available for young people, that they would throw their lives into it, and do whatever it takes to make it happen. So it's sort of self-selecting. Once school started we realized we needed to hire more staff. So then we had to have an election, because that's how staff get hired [after the school is operational].

In the beginning we talked about K and J volunteering, at least for the first couple of months. We set ourselves a deadline at about the end of the second month. People who were interested in becoming full-time paid staff, or paid staff of any amount, could come and the school would be open and they could get to know the kids.

So people were out there looking for staff. Who else can be staff? One founder wanted "erudite people" running the school, not "just moms". He was really against us moms. He had a candidate, a man he knew. Another woman came who was enthralled with the school, and wanted to volunteer. Then another woman came, out of the blue—she must have seen an article. She came and brought all her stuff one day. And R was interested in full-time. All these people said they were interested, so we had four candidates. These people were supposed to come on a regular basis, every week. J and K weren't going to run. But all these people who said they were interested in being staff often would not show up, yet the founding group still went ahead with the whole process of hiring them, and we got to the point of almost offering them contracts, until we realized we can't be doing this. They're not interested!

We started hiring staff because we didn't see our numbers growing, and we wanted to make this thing as real as possible to parents and kids. Having a staff, as well as a building, sounded like it would make it more real. So we basically started hiring staff person by person. We set up procedures, and we hired two people. As it turned out, one dropped out by the summer, when our promised pay started sliding. The other blew up the first week of school. He didn't work out; he was irresponsible. He showed up the second week, came two hours late, and didn't stay the whole day.

We had this early emphasis on staff because we had a lot of parents coming in, listening to us, and I got the impression they liked the idea, but they wanted to find out more about the implementation here. They liked the philosophy, but who are the people involved? Who's my kid going to be talking to? And who's going to be looking after the building? Who's going to be there? So we felt that it makes the whole promise a lot more tangible if you have a real building, real couches, real books, and real people.

In March we scrapped our old staff hiring policy. We had to set up some sort of system, rather than just happening to find somebody and interviewing them, and hiring them, and then waiting and maybe somebody else would show up. So we set up an election procedure, interviewed a lot of people for the full-time and part-time staff positions, and ended up with elections in May and June.

We should have required people to be a founder before being eligible to be on staff initially. I would want to see that sort of commitment, before I would say you could be an original staff person.

The interviewing process produced several cuts. Somebody who wanted to be on staff had to interview with everybody, in groups of two or three of us at a time. Then we would give thumbs up or thumbs down. For the people who survived that, there was election. We had a lot of candidates coming into the interview process, and got rid of several, during that process; and then got rid of several others in the election. Actually, as it turned out, we didn't have a surplus of qualified people.

One of the mistakes we made with the two early people who didn't work out, was that while evaluating these people we gave too much emphasis to a) do they bring certain talents that we don't have?; and b) are they non-establishment? Instead we should have found out if they understand this philosophy; and will they fit in here?

In the early '90's, as part of an on-going correspondence between Sudbury Valley and a start-up group on the west coast, the following letter was written based on Sudbury Valley's twenty-five years of experience (at the time);

The staff for the beginning of the school—and a large part of it for a long time to come—should be drawn from people who have demonstrated a commitment to the ideas and have been a strong part of the working group from as early as they possibly can be. Thus, the people who are now offering themselves as staff candidates should be demonstrating their qualifications by active participation in, and constant attendance at, meetings; participation in the work of committees; and most especially in hard work: not just conceptual work, but very concrete work. They should be doing site searches, they should be working on equipment and furniture, they should be addressing envelopes, doing interviews and making themselves available for meeting the public. Once the site is in line, they should be painting and hammering and making sandwiches. They should be haunting the used furniture stores, and hauling more stuff around in their cars and trucks than fits. This should be the most exciting idea they have heard for many years, and the most fabulous opportunity to be in on the ground floor of creating an institution on the cutting edge of education.

*It is of utmost importance that the selection of the staff not be focussed on teaching. This is not to say that a person should be disqualified for having taught. Far from it. But "teachers" are not what you are looking for. Good adult role models, whether teachers or not, are what you are looking for. People who are dynamic, intelligent, hard workers and **who enjoy the company of children**, and who have a strong moral and ethical sense. Instruction is very far down the list of tasks that you should worry about. Nothing will amaze you more than how unimportant formal instruction is and how important the ability to communicate with children **as human beings** is. And you should most especially beware of people who are still inside the public school system. They are very unlikely to have made the fundamental shift in their heads and hearts that is necessary in order to get Cascade Valley going.*

So, I urge you not to worry about 'pied pipers.' The kids will find all of you and all the work that you do attractive, stimulating and challenging. Charisma is of much less importance than stamina and dedication.

We have always been dedicated to a principle we have called 'self-elimination.' It is a very simple concept and has been almost universally applicable through the life of the school. If the institution isn't right for the person, they will see it, and they will eliminate themselves. And nothing can possibly show it to them better than making tremendous amounts of work necessary, without any pay until school starts! They must become active members of the planning group if they expect to educate themselves enough to be constructive staff members, and wish the institution to consider them as seriously committed. Of course, it is also assumed that there are ongoing sessions to discuss the philosophy and that anyone interested in being a staff member will take part.

I think you will find that the people who care stay with it, and the people who are toying with the ideas do not. Which is just what you want. Now, in order to do it this way, you must decide to postpone consideration of who should become staff members until very much later—into the summer, I would guess. A new institution requires extremely deep commitment, and the planning period should strike everyone interested in working at the school as the most exciting and creative period. If not, they will self-eliminate by not being willing to do the work now.

So far we have focussed on the way a new school gets staffed. We have not addressed the deeper question of what a staff member does or what staff is for. This question is dealt with at length in the literature provided in the Planning Kit, in particular in *The Sudbury Valley School Experience*, in the staff packet in the Kit, in *The 1996 Collection*, and in the book *Reflections on the Sudbury School Concept*. This literature deals with such fundamental questions as what exactly staff needs to be able to do in order to increase the likelihood of success for the school.

Where do the first students come from?

During the period when the founders are working on getting a school going there are usually only a handful of prospective students within the group. Some may be founders, others children of founders. No school seems to get going without some people among the founders who are planning to be students or parents. But throughout the formative period, it is impossible to get a real sense of who the student body might be because so few parameters have been determined about the school. It is a rare parent who will make a real commitment to a school that does not yet have concrete form.

Action begins in earnest on the enrollment front when the school has a site, a staff, and a definite opening date. Before then, one cannot even be totally sure of the students among the founding group. After these things are in place, a nerve-wracking waiting game begins. Hopefully, the p.r. recruitment efforts that the founders have been making will begin to bear fruit in this period. There is, however, no way of knowing who will come and when, and the only sensible policy is to count on very few students and be prepared for more.

It is difficult to overstate how chancy initial enrollment is. In some instances very few students show up at all, and the school either decides it cannot make it with so few, or sweats out the first year until more slowly dribble in. In some instances, a bunch of students show up in the few days before and the few days after school opens. Occasionally a group is lucky enough to have its initial target number of students in advance of opening.

A word of caution: no matter how enthusiastic someone seems to be about enrollment, no matter how sincerely they seem to have committed themselves to coming, no student can be considered to be enrolled until their papers and their tuition are in hand. And even then, when all seems to be in place, you must be prepared for some students or parents making an early departure because, despite your best efforts to explain what the school is about, they were expecting something different. Indeed, this has occurred in almost every school opening situation.

What kind of motivation can be expected to lead families to be among the first to enroll children in a new Sudbury school? If you are lucky, there will be a good-sized contingent who are there because they are enthusiastic about their children being in charge of their own lives; in other words, families who specifically want to be associated with the kind of institution the founders are setting up. It is everybody's dream to have a school in which this is true of virtually the whole community.

Unfortunately, in this connection appearances are often deceiving. Many who talk the talk end up finding it too hard to walk the walk. Many parents see themselves as fully trusting their kids, and as believing in extending a full panoply of rights and freedoms to their children. This turns out to be especially true of so-called "un-schoolers", parents who homeschool their children in a manner that allows a great deal of choice. All too often, however, when these parents are confronted with the fully-operational commitment to individual self-determination that a Sudbury school provides as a matter of principle, they find themselves unable to relinquish their role as custodians of their children's development. Founders must be prepared to deal with repeated disappointment when the initial excitement and pleasure that such families exhibit turn into disillusionment, and often anger. The end result is that only some fraction of those who appear to be in tune with the school's philosophy end up committing to continuing enrollment.

Each new school gets a number of students whose families are looking for something different than what they have already. Usually there are big problems with the child's current situation, and the parents are hoping for some improvement. Most of these people don't really care what the philosophy is, as long as you seem willing to be flexible and are willing to accept their child. A constant problem with these students is that the overwhelming majority of them cannot come to view the school as a real school for "normal" kids simply because the school accepted them! These children are very likely to have "normal" siblings in public schools who are "doing alright". Children who come with this background tend to look at the school as a remedial institution rather than as a healthy community. Sometimes, these families turn out to be the bedrock of the school, its firmest and loudest supporters. Usually, most of the students that come that way are delightful people who are fine to have around as long as their parents allow them to be there.

So you can see that a new school is as likely as not to have three populations with three different perspectives on the school: one, a group that is looking for a Sudbury school; second, a group that thought it was looking for a

Sudbury school until it saw one, and now realizes it wants a Sudbury school with "just a few modifications"; and third, a group that is looking for some sort of refuge from prior unpleasant schooling experiences.

It takes all kinds to make a school, and the first and third group above are the least problematic. The challenge, as we will see, is to create a coherent culture out of whatever mix comes along.

The challenge of creating a coherent culture out of whatever mix comes along also applies to the mix of ages in the original student body. In the ideal world, there would be a number of kids that were little, a number of teenagers, and some in between. The Sudbury literature deals extensively with the advantages of age-mixing, something that has even entered the consciousness of mainstream education. Unfortunately, no matter how hard you try to appeal to parents of different age students in your promotion, there is no way of providing in advance for an ideal age-mix.

Different schools deal with this situation differently. Some luck out and get a pretty good age-mix to start. Schools that know they can only enroll a limited number may set quotas for different age groups in advance, but this can have the result of limiting their total enrollment rather than ensuring a variety of ages. Others struggle for young children, and still others for teens. The problem that these schools have is that once they have a population heavily skewed towards a particular age group, parents of kids in other age groups are discouraged from enrolling their kids by the reality they observe. However, it seems to be less of a problem if the school appears to have lots of young kids, because not only do they grow up eventually, but the fact is that there are tons of desperate teens out there, and the chances are that some of them might land in the school. On the other hand, if a school starts with hardly any young kids, and a lot of pre-teens and teens, it can be very hard to change the situation. Parents of young children tend to be a little frightened of older kids (not totally without reason in the standard school setting) and it is the brave parent who will take the leap of enrolling their little kid before several others have done the same thing.

The nitty-gritty of starting a school

Okay, so the site is pinned down and prepared for use, the staff is lined up, the first students are signed up. All the paper work is in order; the phone is installed; the electricity is buzzing away; there is a filing cabinet (or at least some boxes); there is a computer (or at least some paper and pens). The date for the first day has been set and has arrived.

What do you do now?

Here's how some people describe how they got going:

I remember sitting on the grass talking with students, just hanging out. I worried a lot, answered the phone; I think I tried to reassure parents that it was ok, and perhaps other staff people who didn't have as much certainty or comfort level. Not that my comfort level wasn't completely "blown out of the water" a number of times. But the first day, for a while, I felt pretty comfortable there. I don't really know what I did. Talked with kids, got acquainted, met kids. I get really enthusiastic around kids and can just talk and have fun.

Nobody knew what to do. It was "The Bumbles Start a School".

*One problem we faced was a discussion about a constitution; about **a priori** structure in place before the school starts. We were very close to the beginning. One of the* *founders said, "I think it would be a really good idea to have"—he was always one for wanting to have stuff in place—"a constitution that kids can react to". We had some brainstorming, some getting together about that. He was willing to back off eventually on that, and he said, "Well, we'll see what happens." But he was really concerned because he thought people couldn't handle it if they didn't have some structure to start with. I was going to call Sudbury Valley and talk about it, but I felt that this is the bottom line: we're going to start on day one and ask ourselves, "What are we going to do?" And that first day, in fact, we had a School Meeting and put two laws onto our books. So we really started with a blank slate. We had some problems later, but I never questioned doing it that way.*

The first thing that happened on the first day was—there are two closets, one upstairs and one downstairs. My two girls and I were here first. And there were two vacuums. So they pulled them out and started vacuuming wildly for a half hour, even though the place was spotless. So that was the first thing. Then a couple other people showed up, and they knew each other, but the question finally came out: what do you want to do? So they were looking around, looking around. There's a table that's sort of like a half circle for little kids, and there's a teacher spot there. And they were kind of sitting around that room and they set up a couple chairs and one of them said, "I know what we can do. Let's play school!" So they all sat down for the next hour or two, and they played school!

We had so much stuff to do on basic facilities work, like getting the bookshelves and cleaning the floor and stuff like that, that we never had time to really plan too much for opening day. As far as setting stuff out for kids to do the first day, we didn't have time. But our vision was that we were going to have a facility that had computers ready to roll and so forth, despite the fact that another school had advised us point blank, "Don't put out anything that you don't want trashed." Now I think he's right. If you don't have responsibility, you don't think too much about what's going to happen.

Our focus had been on the facility. Fixing it up, and figuring out what the kids were going to do. Getting activities set up, and materials laid out, and doing much more conventional kinds of thinking about gathering things: what are the basic things that people needed in order to be here—art things and stuff like that, that wouldn't be directing them, exactly, but would be providing them with all these opportunities. Then when we rethought the whole thing, we started putting everything away. We just gathered everything up and said we have to have somebody responsible for these things before we lay them all out. The few things that we left out, without the supervision of a corporation or some sort of structural responsibility, have been just trashed. We have one cupboard, and it's trashed because it just gets thrown back in there. Now nobody does anything with it.

On the other hand, I think that maybe if you're starting a Sudbury type school, the basic structures should be there in some form. I think it's vital to talk to real, live people who are involved in a real, live school. That was absolutely invaluable to us. We visited a neighboring school on Thursday before the Tuesday school opened. They said, "You don't have any rules? Are you crazy? You don't even know if you're going to be a Sudbury school. Who knows what you're going to evolve into. You're going to have a year of chaos." After visiting them, we said, "Hey, they're right. We're pretty stupid, aren't we?" And so we spent several intense days preparing a version of a Lawbook, dealing with issues like, "we don't want to impose this thing on the kids", so we stripped out the behavior rules, because one of the founding kids pointed out that it looked like we were in fact imposing them. We got our founding group to approve it on Sunday night.

I could see the objection: "what were we doing without the kids?" But we'd done all the stuff to set up the school before the kids came—the official authorities stuff, the admissions stuff, and the office stuff. We might as well do it overtly rather than covertly. We might as well say: "This is what's set up. We're doing this temporarily; these are the clerkships, this is what we've done." As one staff member said, "These kids signed up to go to a Sudbury Valley type school. That's what they want, that's what they expect, and so to impose a judicial system and a School Meeting and these clerkships on them, is what they thought they wanted, so it isn't that much of an imposition. And if they don't like some part, they can change it anyway."

We're pretty content with where we did start.

There is no formula, but certain features are apparent. Since you are starting a school with no agenda for activities, then the only way to start is with no agenda for activities.

This means that the first day will inevitably be awkward. For the most part the fun of getting to know one another will be the order of the day, and the students will be working hard on figuring out what they want to do. They will also be carefully watching whether the adults really mean to keep their noses out of the students' affairs, and looking for clues that after all the adults *do* have an agenda. What is amazing is how quickly this process gels; usually by the *second* day, there is a marked relaxation of the atmosphere, and by the end of the first week, the students are showing the first glimmerings of trust that the school is what it said it would be. Hopefully the staff is developing that trust too.

A taste of what the third day of a new school might be like was provided by a founding staff member in a letter to a friend:

> *What I did at work last Wednesday:*
> *After I unlocked and set things up for the day, I had a long conversation with an early-arriving student about books and parents and public education. . . I read up on Robert's Rules. . . I talked with groups of students about the issue of the day, the complaint/observation by our landlord of seeing small children (Who knows if they were ours? We think not) by the fishing lake. . . I played an intellectually taxing, yet enjoyable, card game with a 5-year-old, who has picked up the game more quickly and plays better than most people three or four (or more) times her age. . . with more little kids, I played Rock/ Paper/Scissors, among other more-or-less open-ended games. . . I certified a few people to answer the school phone. . . I took a phone call from someone wanting information—someone who had heard about us through*

a conversation at a beauty parlor. . . I watched and helped (maybe a little) our School Meeting secretary as she typed up the Record for this week. . . a student asked me to proofread a permission slip she'd written for our upcoming trip to an amusement park. . . I stored and inventoried a bunch of office and medical supplies I had purchased for the school. . . I helped sort the mail. . . I looked over some math books as one of our founders explained to me their various levels of difficulty. . . . . .and of course many, many other things I quickly forgot I had done. What an incredible rush it has been, a chaotic and exhilarating and joyful feeling, to see the philosophy and our many months of effort take concrete, exuberant form! Although we as a staff are still feeling our way around, of course, I already feel that it's less a "job" (though of course it involves mountains of work) than it is a matter of simply living (or would that be living simply? hmmm. . .). How busy and challenging and meaningful it is, this job where I "do nothing." How humane, how real. Watching as the students explore their surroundings; as they play and work and talk; as they work out the business of getting along in a smallish space and running their own community and lives, has been every bit as exciting as I had hoped.

So here's to continued joyful struggling, serious play, etc. etc. . .

The most ticklish question of the first days is that of adult intervention. No one questions that adults have a duty to intervene promptly if dangerous or violent situations develop. The hairier issues have to do with behavior that looks questionable to various members of the community. *It is critical to get the School Meeting into the picture, one way or another, as soon as possible.* Whether the school starts with no rules, or with a partial, temporary Lawbook instituted by the founders, the sooner the School Meeting shows itself to be the true governing authority in the community, the more quickly the school will establish itself as a valid institution. There is no task that is more difficult than that of the adults in the opening days. They have to show incredible restraint in their actions while at the same time being forthcoming in the honesty of their interactions. They have to refrain from trying to impose their authority by virtue of being adults, but at the same time be open and blunt with each other and with the students in expressing their honest opinions about the various issues that come up in the opening days of the school. The beauty of the Sudbury is that the School Meeting provides a forum where adults and children alike can speak their minds forcefully in the context of a structure where it is clear that no one person has more say than another in the outcome. The institution of the School Meeting thus renders unnecessary the kind of arm-twisting or brow-beating that would be necessary for the establishment of an orderly community without this structure.

One of the interesting things is that the vagueness and chaos of the beginning days is quickly forgotten as people start to get their lives in order. So, despite the anxiety everyone feels on opening day, when people are later asked to describe what happened, very few remember many details of the initial aimlessness. The message is: get through it; stick to your guns; and somehow convince yourself that before long the school will develop its own internal sense of order.

Developing a culture:
keeping the school going

Once the school is open, the challenge is to keep the school in operation as a Sudbury school possessing its own unique culture. To do this requires a clear understanding of the essential features of such a school, features which define it as belonging to this model, versus what the Greeks would call the "accidental" features, which can vary widely from school to school without adversely affecting its basic character.

This distinction is easy to draw in extreme cases. For example, if a parent comes in and complains about the absence of regularly scheduled, undemanded reading classes, it is clear that they are looking for features which are absolutely alien to the model. If someone complains that the building is not being swept often enough, that is a subject that might call for action—or explaining that the School Meeting likes it that way! But much of the time the issues are grayer. There is no clearcut answer to a parent asking, "Why aren't you being more responsive to my child's expressed interest in chemistry?" So much depends upon the context in which the question is asked: is the interest that of the child or that of the parent? Has the interest in fact been expressed at school, or has the parent been misinformed? Is the school prepared to respond to a genuine request in that area of interest? Is the interest one that actually only appears when the usual delights of the school day are over? Is the parent complaining about the school's lack of eagerness to stimulate student interests or to seize "teaching moments"? These kinds of questions are struggled with throughout the life of the school, but they are hardest to deal with the first year when everybody—founders, staff, parents, students—is just starting to understand and experience what the model is really about. People's confidence is shakiest in that period; there is no live experiential proof of the pudding yet; and the ability to answer such questions is not yet refined.

Much has been written about the subject—in a sense the whole corpus of the SVS Press deals with it. Reading and re-reading parts of that corpus helps; having frequent meetings, especially of staff, to discuss issues as they arise in the daily life of the school helps; having informal get-togethers which are clearly aimed at parents helps; conversing with staff in established schools helps; and in-depth discussions on the School Meeting floor as specific problems arise helps. All this takes time, patience, persistence, strength of character and determination. There is no rest for the weary, not in the first year, for sure, and most likely not in the tenth or twentieth. Though no amount of talking will make people who do not trust their children begin to, there is a tremendous amount of benefit to the school in meeting problems as a group. This helps enormously to build a culture.

One thing that should be anticipated and is rarely avoided is one or more severe crises in the early life of the school precipitated by parents (and occasionally by staff) who become angry when they discover that the model in action differs from what they thought it would be when they decided to participate, and who seek to change the school to fit their own conception. It is not unusual for these people to feel that they have been betrayed—that *their* fantasy should have been the reality, and the reality that has developed is a malicious perversion perpetrated by the dominant majority. Feelings run extraordinarily high because people's children are involved and their egos and their world views are threatened. When these splits occur, the result is deep upheavals in the community. People on the periphery of the vortex of discontent are puzzled by its intensity and annoyed at its disruptiveness. The school often loses not only the malcontents, but also often others who want to escape an atmosphere of violent disagreement and poisonous anger.

We say all this not to be discouraging but to try to prepare people for a likely reality. Sudbury Valley was torn asunder twice during its first year, and once again shaken at the end of its second decade. Of the first twenty Sudbury schools to be founded after Sudbury Valley, at least thirteen are known to have gone through devastating crises, as have several groups that have either disbanded or not yet opened. The odds are high for it to happen, so count your blessings (and fasten your seat belts) as long as you have succeeded in avoiding it.

Aside from the general set of traditions and shared experiences that slowly give form to a community and define its culture, two specific features of Sudbury schools play a central role in giving each school its unique flavor: the judicial system and the School Meeting. The judicial system develops the experiential base for the community's sense of fairness and justice, as well as its attitudes towards punishment, rehabilitation, inclusion, exclusion, and the dividing line between personal and communal concerns. The School Meeting defines the underlying parameters for these issues, and determines a myriad of other community norms, such as the concept of fiscal responsibility, official accountability, environmental aesthetics, etc.

The judicial process and the School Meeting usually absorb enormous amounts of time during the first few years of the school, sometimes hours a day. No time could be better spent, since these institutions are breathing life into the structures that give the community form. The daily and weekly discussions and debates, the monthly and yearly re-examinations of every facet of the school's existence, are the conceptual and spiritual backbone of the developing community.

Some classic errors

Starting too soon or waiting too long

It is not actually all that useful to warn against starting too soon or waiting too long, because nobody really can tell anyone else when the "right" time is. Technical things do not define the right time. Rather the determination of the founding group and its readiness to open define the right time; and other things tend to fall into place once the time is ripe to open. The key factors that make for readiness include having a coherent founding group with a clear focus about its philosophical aims; clearly understanding, and having enough energy committed to carrying out, the practical work that has to precede opening; having enough seed money committed to get through the opening months; having a core staff assembled that can see the school through its entire first year, regardless of budgetary considerations; and having a reasonable expectation that there will be a student body on opening day.

If any of these key factors is missing, the likelihood for success is diminished. By the end of 1996, to the best of our knowledge, some seven groups opened schools that failed, mostly within the first year or so. An additional five groups that had made significant progress toward starting, and indeed expected to open, had to throw in the towel. Meanwhile, a total of about seventeen schools that can be considered Sudbury schools in their essentials have opened since 1968 and were still in operation. It appears to us that the failures occurred due to the absence of one or more key factors, and that the schools that have continued to operate have done so because, by hook or by crook, they manage to have all the key factors in place, or to get them in place once the need manifested itself.

Allowing for compromise of essentials

Talking about this is like beating a dead horse. It is relatively easy to open an alternative school which is just "a little" different than the Sudbury model—i.e., which compromise enough of the essential features of the model to satisfy the anxieties of parents who still accept the major premises of the mainstream model. For example, if you should decide to offer a smorgasbord of courses, or to "stimulate the students' interests", or to make sure that every child learns "the basics", or to monitor students' progress and report it back to the parents, or to guarantee staff presence in all student activities, then you are much more likely to get the backing you need to start a school. You may find yourself qualifying for grants, or for public school charter status. And plenty of parents will be happy to pay tuition for such a school.

You will also find that you have in fact started an alternative school, which is quite an achievement in its own right, but it will be missing some of the key features of a Sudbury school.

Slavishly following Sudbury Valley School

The flip side of leaving out some of the essentials is insisting that every detail conform to the practice in Sudbury Valley School or in one of the other established schools.

Rather than going through the hard work of establishing your own culture, sometimes it is tempting to try to adopt-a-culture, especially because the one you wish to adopt seems to work so well. This temptation is especially strong when you realize how exhausted you are from the effort of getting a school under way, and how hard it is to create a culture.

To be sure, it is often reasonable to seek out, or point to, the experience of other Sudbury schools when a problem surfaces in yours. That information is always helpful in the decision-making process, but only if you are willing to sift out what is really relevant to your own community and create solutions that are appropriate to your own unique conditions.

Over-dependence on home-schoolers to populate the school

It is tempting to think of homeschoolers—especially those who call themselves "unschoolers", who aim to give their children complete freedom to do as they wish with their time—as a natural target market for students for a Sudbury school. Indeed, often homeschoolers are very excited about the idea of such a school opening in their area, and they often have time to be helpful and even instrumental in the set-up period.

Unfortunately, there are many things about your school that may not please many homeschoolers, even unschoolers, that may not be obvious at first blush. Thus, in the absence (or even presence) of seeing the model in operation, some people understand the explanation of such a school to mean that it is a place where students choose the time and place to do whatever *studying* they wish to do. (Of course, that is one of the facets of the school.) They do not wish their children to be coerced, but they assume that the atmosphere of the school will be one that "promotes" specific academic pursuits, rather than one that treats all pursuits as equally valid. Or, even after learning a great deal about the model you are following, some unschoolers are likely at some point—either before or after opening—to become uncomfortable because the school, though it may have a very likable group of people associated with it, is not a sufficiently warm and protective environment; the staff is not providing "enough" exposure; instruction is not available unless it is actively sought; students consistently pursue activities without adult supervision; there are certain influences that the children might come under that the parents consider "unsavory"—like playing video games, or maybe even watching television; etc. The central problem is a control problem: homeschooling students, in even the most benign circumstances, are pretty much under the watchful eye of the adults around them. Kids at Sudbury schools have no adults supervising or taking responsibility for their progress and development.

There is another interesting aspect of many homeschooling situations: the children tend to be more dependent on their parents, or on adult direction, than most kids, so they are not the most likely candidates to form the portion of the community that is most independent and has most self-direction. As one school founder put it: "We get some students who have been homeschooled. We don't want to shut out that group, but it's not the rich, fertile field one might imagine for prospective students. The parents have often raised kids who are extraordinarily self-centered past the age of two and a half, when it's appropriate to be that self-centered."

It is a fact that former homeschoolers have participated successfully and happily in virtually every Sudbury school. Founding groups should however be alert to the potential problems that might face them if, in the formative period, they rely exclusively, or overwhelmingly, on homeschoolers as the backbone of a new Sudbury school.

What people feel enabled them to succeed

All of the foregoing has been an attempt to outline factors that enhance, or decrease, the likelihood of success when trying to found a Sudbury school. We would like to end with some comments make by founders of schools that succeeded in opening when asked to describe the key elements that made it possible for them to go from conception to realization. Here is what some of them said.

The reason I think it took off is just enough people were ready for it. Really ready, and willing to get it going. I was able to do everything that was required up until March. Then in March, just when the workload would have been impossible, in terms of all the stuff about getting the facilities ready, all the PR events we needed to do, all the legal stuff we had to do; just when I could not have possibly done more than a quarter of it, we got an infusion of about six or eight really committed people, who spent an incredible amount of time doing it. People who were as committed as I was. That group carried us from March.

I think the incredibly deep friendship among the founders was a big element in our success. The other thing is that we all believe in the model so strongly and that we want it so badly for our own children. We felt we have to give this our all, and if it doesn't work, it doesn't work. But there's no other alternative that can really compare to this for our kids. I guess there is a cost that would be too much—if it was tearing our families apart. It's been stressful, and there have been rough periods when we've said, "This is too much. We can't. It's not worth the price." I think we've come close to throwing in the towel, but we always look at the opposite side of the coin, as it were, and just keep plowing.

Why did we succeed? I really cannot honestly say we deserved it. I wish that I could say it was because of our superior skill or something. We just gave it everything we could, and it worked out beyond what we deserved, really. That's how I feel about it. So I'm really grateful; there's a certain amount of good karma, or luck, or just something happening beyond what we could do. Because it really seems like what we did was impossible.

Two of us were the source of this thing being here, and in the beginning, if you lose the source, then the thing disappears. We're still important as the source, ongoingly, but we're not the only source of it now. I don't know what would happen if we disappeared from the school, but at least it would have a chance. It's really a shift, it's clear. It was a little hard for me, in that when we were the sole source, we had at least the illusion that we had some control over what was happening, and we really lost that. We really do not have control over this now. I think it is like when your children leave home and you're no longer needed as a parent, your role is changed.

I've seen other organizations develop, and I see what makes them strong. What happens in the beginning really makes a tremendous difference: making the roots really strong, and having as much integrity as you can. Keeping integrity throughout the whole thing, whatever challenges and problems you have. It's like a tree. The key part of its strength is how deep the roots go. If the roots are shallow, the tree can get tall, but it's going to topple eventually. But if you get deep roots, it's going to be stable. It's going to really make a difference.

To some extent, I think our success had to do with just the idea itself. When G. came back from Sudbury Valley, I knew she was "infected", and I, by contagion, got it. And H., as another ingredient in this chemical reaction here, was already a chronic case. So I really think that a lot of it was the three of us really committing to making it happen. That's my sense, looking back on it. The three of us have really handled the major onslaught of outside forces. I think that's the necessary and sufficient energy. We formed that kind of blueprint that made it happen.

I think we succeeded because of two things. I think it was because we had trust in each other. Like I always knew that if K. had a task, it was going to happen. I never doubted that. And similarly each one of us divvying up the work, there was that trust that people were going to follow through. We could rely on each other to stay committed, to stay involved, to do the work that was necessary. The second thing is that we had the crucial number, whatever that crucial number is, but enough people so no one was overwhelmed. Enough people so that the work could be divided, for each person's individual strengths and proclivities. The balance worked.

H. held the vision of this model of school. If we ever said, "Whoa, is that going to really happen that way?"

he would say, "yeah." He would always be able to explain our vision to us if we got lost.

We sort of steered the ship in the right direction and bounced off enough rocks to get where we are. We had none of the skills to sound out the way ahead, or to have the peripheral vision to see the things that were lurking in the shadows. We had an overwhelming sense of vision of where we wanted to go, and a kind of a compass direction on how to get there. But the rest of it, all of the minutiae, things like complying with codes—we didn't really have a good sense of that. But we learned; it was on-the-job training.

Some of the best advice that we got was from frantic calls to Sudbury Valley: "Has this ever happened to you?" To us it seemed like pearls of wisdom coming down the pipe, and that was our saving grace. "Oh, yeah, that happens to us all the time." If I had to advise somebody starting, I'd say, go to an existing school. Go to more than one existing school, because they all do it differently. The first thing you have to do is the research. You have to read. You have to read all those books. You really do. And if you make it through that ordeal (if you're not already in that mindset, in which case it is not a choice) then the books might put you over the edge enough to either leave the group or join it.

That's where it starts. Read the books, get the information, then make your decisions. The first decision you have to make is do you want to be a Sudbury school? We had this vast resource of experience in Sudbury Valley, and we felt we'd be fools if we didn't at least try not to make the same mistakes. We don't have to reinvent the wheel, we'll just go to the source. We'll read and find out the information that's necessary to get from point A to point B. Then at point B we'll make the decision on whether to go to point C. It was a methodical step by step kind of thing. We didn't just jump in and do everything in the first couple of months. It took a year and a half worth of groaning and complaining. The first year was doing all of this questioning and research and looking at all the options and narrowing them down. Then the last six months was finally when we had that vision and decision: this is what we want to do. This particular school, Sudbury Valley, works, and has worked for a number of years. It's gone through some changes in its history, and why should we be doomed to repeat their mistakes? Why don't we adopt as much of this that works, and will work for us, and go from there? It's like buying a house. Who buys a house that is exactly what they want? It doesn't happen in the real world. You buy a house that you see potential in, and you figure you can live comfortably in while you remodel it to be what you want. Isn't that the way it works?

The school survived on M.'s acumen. It's not acumen that has to do with money. It has to do with having a vision of what the school's supposed to be all about, and sticking with it. I think that was essential. Her vision, and her sense of what direction this group needed to go in—"excuse me, why are there so many questions about it? Why are we dithering?"

There was a sense that M. brought, that I took strength from more than once, which was that there were certain things that you just didn't compromise on. That was sort of the gauntlet, the line in the sand. For me, her influence had to do with painting a fairly clear picture—the vision thing—and you either see it and you agree with it, or you don't.

Otherwise it would have been this sort of amorphous thing that kind of wallowed around and didn't stand for anything. Those kinds of organizations die. They either die immediately, or they die some sort of boring death as time goes on. And this group just sort of cut off that part that was always gonna be outside pissing in. We needed them inside pissing out.

In addition, during the first year, particularly, a lot of people put in a lot of incredible hours. An extraordinary number of honorable, step up to the plate, people were involved. There were many people who fell out around incidentals, but there were some core principles of right action, or love for democracy, or patriotism, or whatever you want to call it, that time after time came through. We saw some nobility, as well as some of the more ignoble parts of human nature. I have a fairly sappy view of it.

Appendix 1

An account of the trials and tribulations of a founder whose school survived only a few months, and who alone carried most of the burden of setting it up and sustaining it.

Working at creating a school like SVS is causing me to put the pieces together, to create from my own experience a perspective I can define and share with others. The philosophy of SVS seems so simple to me, so easy, I can't understand why it's difficult for others to comprehend. At the beginning of my little adventure, I was afraid I would rant and rave and shout, "Don't you get it?" Instead, I'm listening a lot, and watching how the mind works, and sometimes the heart. And it seems that when the heart's been reached, a little light goes on, then understanding comes.

People ask me why they haven't heard of SVS, why there aren't similar schools all around. *Aspects of Creating and Replicating a New Model*[4] explains it all very neatly, as discouraging as it is. Most people are very generous with discouragement; most think I shouldn't even try to start a school, and I certainly shouldn't try to do it here. Here I am anyway.

---

[4] *Reflections on the Sudbury School Concept*, (Sudbury Valley School Press, Framingham, MA, 1999) p. 303.

Because I was blessed enough to be a student at SVS, I tell people I don't have to make any leaps of faith. My parents did. My sister, home from college for the weekend, sat at the dining room table and said to my mother "let her go. She'll be fine." It's all we need to do for all of our children. What surprises me the most is that people don't *want* to hear about change, honest change. I've had some conversations, too brief and maybe I should have tried to take them further, where I can see the other person shut off. They listen a little, decide the whole idea is crazy (or I am), and stop listening. Even when offered SVS's documented history of success, they still don't want to think about it.

Part of the problem in explaining and understanding the SVS way is that shared experience is too often thoughtless experience. People have grown up in a world defined for them by others. The definitions are the same for everyone, and the prevalent attitude is, "If it was good enough for me, it's good enough for my children," and, "That's the way it is." People don't intend harm, at least I hope they don't. They are guilty of not being *thoughtful*. In the fall, when my gorgeous, intense, energetic daughter came home from every day of first grade in a tantrum-trance state, when she couldn't be touched or spoken to, a friend remarked, "Oh, first grade is 90 days of PMS. It happens to everyone." She saw humor in it. Needless to say, I didn't.

So I reach out to people, anyone who'll listen really, anyone who thinks they might be looking for something different, and I try to explain.

"What is the curriculum?"

I used to say, "There is no curriculum." Then I said, "There is no defined curriculum." Now I say, "The curriculum is limited only by the imagination of the child."

A school without a curriculum can't be imagined. When "school" is heard, people can only think of their idea of school, or their own experience of school. "Curriculum" is something concrete, something that can be imagined and something that people can believe in changing in order to change the bigger picture. First, "curriculum" conjures images, then those images have to be looked at, and allowed to fade away, to become something other. Unfortunately, the image of children being allowed to be who they are implies anarchy. Children in control of their own lives, or honestly moving "at their own pace" is fairly horrifying to some. What people see when they think of "moving at one's own pace" is really "moving at one's own pace as long as it fits in the schedule." The same happens with the ideas of assessments and evaluations. It's deeply ingrained that we must measure and evaluate; not doing so hangs beyond the imagination. For a while.

I have watched one mother come to an understanding of the SVS way. When I first met her, she was wound so tightly I thought she would explode. She's the mother of two sons in public school, her first son measuring up to the standards of "genius" (whatever that means) and not functioning — the way the school wants him to. Of course, the school tells this poor mother that the son must be forced, must be drilled, must be made to perform. In her heart of hearts she knows his way is different, and that he's not getting what he needs, but she was surrounded by people whose only experience is the traditional way. Their ideas are so entrenched in the only way they know, that anything other can't be imagined.

Then she met me (blessing or curse, who knows?). She borrowed books and tapes, came to the meetings. It took about two months for the light to come on, and come on it did. As difficult as it will be for her to afford a private school, I expect she'll be one of our strongest supporters.

One of the mothers at our first meeting was truly horrified to read that "only" fifty percent of SVS graduates attend college after. *[Editor's note: An incorrect statistic, reported in Boston Globe. Actually about 80% go on to further education.]* Another man tossed in, "You know, we don't notice it because we live in the suburbs, but fifty percent of our children drop out of school." (Bless him.)

"I want my children to go to college," she said.

But what if they want something else?

Understanding SVS raises more that our ideas about education. We have to reach way in there, and look at our own notions and images and experiences as individuals, then as parents, then through our children's eyes as well. It may be easier for some to allow others to make those definitions. It never was for me.

One of the worst aspects of my years in public school was having others define for me my experience of the world. (I didn't finish with that one until I was thirty years old. It was those childbirth preparation classes. Every one of those old buttons was being pushed, and I was wild.) I have images of myself at various young ages, standing stupefied, listening to a teacher going on and on, me believing none of it and thinking this person doesn't live on the planet I live on. And we don't all live on the same planet. We live on little, tiny, homey planets that belong to us alone, and every planet is worthy of being honored, and of not being violated. Too much is lost if we allow others to define us, or our little planets.

It's interesting to me that most of the people who call are the mothers. Most of the mothers are the primary caretakers, and now that I think about it, our group's one man shares equally in looking after his son. The mothers know, in their heart of hearts, that their children are bright and beautiful, wonderful little people. The kids start school, things start falling apart, mothers start looking around for something different.

Most are trying to work within the system. I thought I might end up working with the system too, through a charter school. I thought it would be great. Here we have a long-standing successful model; the school would be local and public; and the state would work with us in finding a site. It didn't take very long to discover that the charter would never be granted. Charter school students have to meet the same standards and fulfill the same requirements as public school students. *It's written into the law* [in my state]. The state and some of its people are looking for change, it's true, but while they'll change the details, with great effort and expense, they won't let go of the old standards, the old ideas and images. Their world is defined for them.

Progress is very slow in getting the word out and getting people to move. I know that time has to pass for people to come to an understanding of the SVS way, but I'm also getting impatient. This small group I've gathered may be interested in creating something different, or having something different available, and be unwilling to make the commitment.

I understand why SVS has chosen to look after itself the way it has. I won't bang my head against that wall either. This school, if and when it happens, will be a private, democratic, free-standing school simply because it has to be. There is no other way.

Appendix 2

Narrative history of a school that has succeeded in surviving its first four years

In the fall of 1991, N., who lives in a place we shall call Smalltown, read an article about Sudbury Valley in *Mothering Magazine*. She began to discuss the article with others—aggressively; some might say by 'buttonholing'. At the time, N. was home schooling her children, ages 9 and 7, and had been looking into joining an unschooling group in a nearby city. She is active in town affairs, and has had a lot of experience in community organizing around specific causes. She was also operating a bookstore; her husband is a physician.

The median income in the area in the mid '90s was about $29,000; median home value, about $80,000. About 20% of the community are upper middle class people who work in the state capital, which is contiguous to Smalltown, and most of the rest are blue collar workers, many of whom are involved in rural industries. The area is also a center for some modern back-to-the-land families. Smalltown's population is 7,000, and the entire area has a low population density. It is about 1 hour from the nearest large city. There is no tradition of alternative education, and little of private education—not even many Christian schools.

Among the people given the article by N., was K., a colleague of N.'s in the Historical Society, whose husband works for the State Department of Education and who has a graphic design business.

She came rushing over to my house and she said, "K.,
you've got to read this. This is incredible." And I said,
"OK, I will" . . . What was my response? I think N.
had been enthusiastic about . . . I mean, the bookstore
was wonderful, and we would go in and she would say,
"This book is fantastic!" So this is her pattern.

N. also saw John Gatto on the McNeil-Lehrer show, and he mentioned Sudbury Valley. She became obsessed with bringing Gatto to her community to shake things up in the establishment. In April, N. went to see Gatto at a nearby homeschooling conference, tried (but failed) to visit Sudbury Valley (because she could not bring children on the visit), met a Sudbury Valley parent at the conference, and began a friendship with her. N. succeeded in bringing Gatto in May. As she put it:

I've always maintained a very good relationship, a
very comfortable relationship, with the school district.
People can shake their heads and say, "She's a nut," but
nobody runs away when they see me. . . I just wanted
people to be aware. Gatto likes to do that. He likes to
fire people up and really get the engines going.

In the fall of 1992, after failing once again to arrange a visit to SVS, even with help from the parent she had met, N. received a complete Planning Kit "on loan" from her friend, and immediately "sucked it all up" and began plying K. with videos and books. Finally, N. came to the twenty-fifth anniversary Alumni Retrospective evening, January 23, 1993, at SVS.

> *The Retrospective pushed me over the edge. I drove home like a madwoman saying, "We've got to do it. We've got to do it." The only reason I didn't go to K.'s house that night was because it was three in the morning. I thought, I can't be beating down her door at this time, but I think it was eight the next morning when I went.*

The reason N. turned to K. first was because "K. and I had talked for hours and hours about education", and also because "she has the writing ability; the kind of things she does will appeal to people; and the graphics and everything." As K. put it:

> *I think probably because I was the most totally enthusiastic person about the earlier articles . . . I didn't have any reservations. Probably other people said, "Oh, yeah, that's really good, but gee, do you think it would really work?" or something like that. I didn't have that response. I seemed like a person who would plunge into it.*

By February 26, the first meeting was organized, at N.'s house, to which some 25 people came. K. had prepared the first brochure in time for this. Meanwhile K. and her husband were on a task force for developing new ideas for Smalltown, along with the Superintendent of Schools. As part of this, K. was hoping to sell the school district on having a small alternative magnet school, hoping to attract kids unhappy with public school, using public funding, similar to Sudbury Valley. The Superintendent was completely uninterested, and this idea got nowhere. K.:

> *I'm not the kind of person who starts things. I read it and say 'yes, it's wonderful, I wish I lived in Framingham.' And that would be the end of it... If N. had come to me and said, "I am going to start a Sudbury model school, would you like your kids to come?" I would have said "Yes", and that would have been the end of it for me. Because I had a whole life... But, she didn't. She said, "I'm going to do this and would you do this with me because I can't do it alone." And I said, "Sure, I'll try."... Little did I know it was going to take over my life.*

In the short period between January 23 and February 26, the decision was essentially taken by N. and K. to go ahead and start a school. The goal was to open in September of 1993.

> *We were very naive. We didn't know what intense personal relationships you would need for this kind of thing. We didn't know whether we could work well together on a long term basis. We didn't know we would need to be able to do that. We didn't know how time consuming it would be. We didn't know how hard it would be. But we also didn't know how wonderful it would be.*

The idea of the February 26 meeting was to get as many people together as possible who were interested in alternative education, and to sift out those who were interested in the Sudbury model. K.:

We'll come to a meeting where we will all hammer out our educational approaches, and our expectations and our hopes, and see who wants what, and what direction or directions to go in. Even if you decide to go with a more traditional, progressive approach, there will be people at the meeting who prefer that, so it will be useful for them as well as for us, and that whole group will go off and they will have their own meeting from then on. We would have a nice little split, a friendly split, right at the beginning. It didn't happen. It probably would have been helpful if we had.

The main practical outcome of the February meeting was to set a date for the a planning meeting, March 29, and for the next large meeting, April 3. A lot of people who seemed very interested at the February 26 meeting faded away, and never showed up again. In between, K. sent a letter reporting on the first meeting and produced the first *New School Newsletter*. They used an enormous mailing list for the second meeting, produced by networking with people on first mailing list.

For the big April 3 meeting, they planned something different: K.:

I thought that we had seen the video, and we had books, and we had articles and we had done a lot of talking, and we did the dumb little flyer. But because this was such a different kind of model and people couldn't quite picture how it would work, I thought we would act it out. We would have two models. We would have people sitting in rows and there would be the bored kid and the kid who threw paper airplanes and the person who was asleep and—it would be funny and amusing.

But getting people to play the roles was difficult. Nobody would play the really negative ones. Throughout the entire history of our school there was tip-toeing around the public schools—not offending them has been a very important issue. On the other hand, we wanted to make it clear why do all this. It was very amusing.

Committees were established at that meeting—public relations, financial, site, philosophy, and a coordinating planning committee, which was the core group. Membership of the committees included four other people. The first meetings of these committees took place during April. They were prepared to open in September, even if they only had their own five kids as students.

In fact, the chief motivation for all of the active members of the founding group was to have a place for their own children. The group was mostly women, and always operated informally, reaching decisions by general consensus. K.: "We didn't have anybody disruptive or abrasive or hostile at our meetings. If we had, I think we would have approached it in a different way." By mid-spring, the really active members of the group were N. and K., who essentially carried the ball (K.: "People were happy to have us do the work. There was nobody who wanted to do the work that we weren't letting do work."), and a few others. One of them was a therapist. K.:

She had a number of issues of concern about the school. She lives in a world of threat and fear, partly because of her job—she deals with lunatics, and the world is a lunatic, frightening, horrible place. [She was afraid] we had a psychotic killer here at the school who was going to kill somebody, and we had asbestos, and we had a little girl who was being savaged by other little girls, issues of general unsafeness. During the first year she came in and said, "I'm going to start a group for kids whose projects just don't fly." Her group didn't fly!

The group's meetings mostly dealt with practical issues. There was little focus on educational philosophy. K.:

We thought early on there would be endless discussions—that we'd have a discussion group a week and we'd get into all this neat stuff, and we'd debate until the small hours of the night and all that. Nobody cared. Nobody was interested. We had several meetings where two people showed up and all they wanted to know about was, "Can you accommodate my kid who is having trouble in high school?"

In May, they got their first publicity, in the form of articles in two different regional newspapers.

Meanwhile, the site committee was looking feverishly for sites. The search extended over several months and included consideration of extremely varied possibilities. One by one the possibilities were eliminated: houses, warehouses, barns, empty schools, all kinds of things. One day an acquaintance of N.'s who had been a school board members suggested they look into an old school building, in the center of Smalltown, which had not been used by the school district for about five years and had been given to the city. N.:

He said 'Why not use that?' I said, "It's terrible; there is asbestos in that building. That building was closed because it is a fire trap." He said, "You know as well as I do that building is workable. The school district didn't

*want it for about five years, so they did nothing except
wash the floors. There was very little maintenance. The
furnace is a mess. The roof is falling in. It's a pit." And it
was being vandalized in a major way. So I went down
and I said to the City Manager "What would be the
possibility of our school renting part of that building?"
And he said, "I don't know; why don't you go up and
look at it." He thought, "This woman is a crackpot."
So he gave me the key and I remember coming in and
standing in the auditorium all by myself and saying,
"This will work. This will work. It's big." And it was
a mess. So I went back to him and said "We would
like to talk about this." But it had to go through the
City Council. I knew some of the Councilors so I called
them up. Several of them are my husband's patients. I
called the head of whatever committee it was and he
said "You're the answer to my prayers. I want to keep
that building going. The city wants to get rid of it. I'll
do whatever I can." And he did. He stood on his head
for us.*
K.:

*In a way, being in a school that looks so schoolish and
traditional legitimized us in people's eyes. Even though
they didn't like the building, and a lot of them said
"Oh, God, it's like when I went to school". But we had
couches, and they'd say, "Oh, it looks like a school, but
it's so warm and friendly". And they never questioned
our credentials.*

In July the rental was arranged and they had a site. The
town also let them use any of the furnishings in the building, like chairs, couches, bookcases, desks, filing cabinets.

Also, people were donating a large number of books, as well as furniture. Even people who were not interested in the school, but had friends that were in the planning group were quite generous. The lease was actually signed on the 16th of August and the first event in the new building was a public meeting on August 19th, at which Mimsy Sadofsky, from Sudbury Valley School, presented a talk. For three days, half a dozen people worked non-stop to get the building in shape for the event. The friendly committee chairman got a city crew to come and remove some of the junk.

Mimsy's visit included an afternoon of staff training with about half a dozen people. She addressed an open house to which about fifty people came, which was announced with a mass mailing, posters and an ad in the paper. Several city officials attended too. The group felt the meeting was a great success. K.:

> It legitimized us, in terms of being respectable and having people from the outside who had done this. Mimsy presented herself very well, and she was professional and educated and literate and friendly. And it was simple.

On August 30, there was another public meeting with prospective parents, and admissions interviews, conducted by people in the core group, were held on September 2. The school opened with about 20 students.

The original staff chose itself. K.: "We were self-selected. 'I'll do it. How about you?' 'Yeah, I'll do it.'" N.: "There was no vote. That I remember." The first year there were five staff members, and when N. pulled out for a period in the spring, due to exhaustion, two more came in as volunteers.

The rate of pay has always been $5 an hour, which could also be used to pay off tuition if a staff member had a child at the school. Most everyone volunteers time in addition to what they are paid for. They do not have contracts.

The first few months were rocky: "Partly it was our inexperience, and partly it was that there were a number of kids at the school who were very unsuitable for the school. But we didn't know that and they didn't know that." There were already deep, but undiscussed, divisions in philosophy among the staff. N.: "We didn't sit down and talk nearly enough in the first year, because we were always doing damage control. It was always the riot squad responding to a situation." On the other hand, according to K.,

> I think dialoguing on philosophical issues would have been counter-productive the first year, and probably still [in the third year]. Because in fact there are two people here who really believe in the model, and the other people just want a nice alternative school, but are willing to go along with us. Philosophical discussions would open up a big can of worms. I mean, we're getting along, they're playing their part in this school. We're very uncomfortable internally, but the school is operating the way it should—but we have to keep pushing, pushing, pushing to keep it on track.

N.: "We're waiting for the bomb to hit." The issue of how closely the school is modeled on Sudbury Valley is, and has always been, thorny. K.:

> Often, in conversation and in School Meeting, issues will come up. And then we say, "Well, this is not the model. This is not how we do it here." Or we say the

*fatal words, "Well, at Sudbury Valley, they do . . ." And
boy, is that always a problem!*
    *Of course, we're not Sudbury Valley. And we're try-
ing to train ourselves not to always say the "SV" words.*

There was trouble with some of the teenage students.
One of them was expelled mid-year, another left with her,
and two more, one male and one female, hung in there till
the end of the year. The first year ended with 18 students;
the second year ended with 21. The third year ended below 20. The school was affected the entire year by a schism
within the staff, and at the end one staff member left, pur-
portedly to found her own school, and took a few students
with her.

After the school opened, open houses were continued
for promotional purposes, although the feeling is that they
are not very productive. During the third year, a large local
fair, which takes place yearly, proved to be a good venue for
advertising. They have also gotten some newspaper coverage, and do some advertising, although it does not seem
to be very effective. Libraries are sporadically stocked with
flyers, and occasional newsletters and announcements are
sent out to a maillist they keep by hand. They have also
written to guidance counselors and superintendents, but
with little feedback. Their first TV coverage was way too
early, but they have been on TV again, and were on a radio
talk show. All in all, word of mouth is their most important vehicle for getting the school known. K.: "People from
the community have been surprisingly nice." N.: "Nobody
runs when they see us."

All of the start up expenses for the school (postage,
copying, flyers, labor) were donated by N. and K. without
keeping any detailed records. They estimate that their out

of pocket expenses were in the vicinity of $800. Founders were never assessed. They earned a little money from a yard sale. All other expense were covered by tuition, and money was managed very carefully. N.: "We don't owe anybody. If we closed tomorrow, we'd pay all the bills and we'd be flat, but [not in debt]." A prospective and a budget were drawn up when the group was considering buying a property, all based on tuition income.

To attract additional students for the second year, late in the summer they instituted a two-tier tuition plan. Returning students paid at the regular rate, and new students were given a sizable discount. Although they seem to have gotten a few new students because of this, they decided not to repeat the experiment. Staff gets paid minimally. In general there is very little money available. K.:

> *I think the perception that the kids have is that, although we talk about how we have to be really careful with money, and we really don't have a lot, they feel comfortable about the flow of money for what they need at the school. If they want $30 for more photography supplies they can have it. And the Art Corporation has a $100 budget.*

Accreditation is an issue. The state accredits private schools, as does the New England Association of School and Colleges. An accredited school is approved for tuition purposes, which means that people who live in towns with no high schools can send their kids to any accredited high school that is willing to accept them and have the state pay the tuition. However there is no stigma to running a school that is not accredited.

Frequent Assembly potlucks have been instrumental in keeping the community on keel, somewhat unified. People get a chance to air their anxieties, but they seem to do it in a very calm way. K.: "The potlucks are kind of weird in a way because everyone sits around and says how wonderful it all is and it seems a little phoney. But apparently they need it; testimonials." The dissension in the school, which has not been insignificant, has focussed in the staff. There have been major problems every year.

The school has always drawn many teenagers and very few young children. They speculate that the building is not very welcoming to small children, but there is no real evidence for this. During the third year, several teens came into their own as strong leaders in the community.

For the first year or so, the school had a judicial committee system, but it always had problems with process and problems gaining the respect of the school community. During the second year, they began to do judicial work within a special Judicial School Meeting. This has worked out much better although it is sometimes cumbersome. Year by year the school has calmed down. In the fall of the third year, N. could say: "We're still in the Wild West, but it is less wild—much, much less wild."

Students who enroll during the year pay pro-rated tuition until the end of the school year. This has meant that many families can "try" the school for a few months, and has been somewhat destabilizing.

Work at the school was much more wearing than the founders anticipated. N.:

There were times during the first year I wanted to pull out. Not because I didn't believe in the model, but because I was really upset about how things were going.

I was impatient. So I had to really look within myself,
talk to people, listen, pray, stand on my head. Then I
came to the point where I needed to regroup: the school
needs me, I need the school, my kids need the school, my
kids don't want to leave. There is no other option. So
I've got to hang in there. . . It's hard work when you're
a person who has been used to calling her own shots and
other people are saying, "No, we don't agree with you."

In addition to the regular stresses, there was a lot of plain
hard work. For six months, N. opened and closed the
school every day, although her colleagues say they would
have been happy to help had they known the stress she was
under. Meanwhile, during most of the school's existence,
K. has been doing a great deal of work for the school on her
computer at home until all hours of the morning.

N. and K. attribute their success to total commitment.
N.: "I think we've succeeded because at least K. and I believe in this 100%."

Appendix 3

Only the Hopeful

Nan Narboe (1996)

With a show of hands, the dozen parents and teachers packed into the supply room of a closed office voted to start a school where children could do what interested them—all of the time. The group had come together because of a common interest in education as it's conducted at Massachusetts' revolutionary Sudbury Valley School. Founder Daniel Greenberg's *Free at Last* and *Schooling without Coercion*, had convinced us. Students should learn what they want to learn, and learn it in a democratic setting.

"Most educational philosophies are either too permissive or too controlling," said one woman, like me, a mother who ended up working at the school. "I could see where they went wrong, but I couldn't see a way to combine freedom with responsibility, until I read about Sudbury."

We wanted what Sudbury Valley School had and we wanted it in Portland, Oregon. We set to work. We brought Greenberg to town to give a speech—a speech so rousing that one man who heard it stayed up all night, then showed up the next day to work on the school. We adopted Sudbury's bylaws as our own, then met weekly, Sundays at three, to compare notes and make decisions. We studied state law. We borrowed money, located a site, set tuition, and chose staff, all by majority rule.

We held events to attract potential students. Obstacle after obstacle gave way. Proudly we set the date for our school to open, Cascade Valley School, the school we all wanted.

Then the students arrived—and our troubles began. The previously unified group fissured into difference after difference. The language we shared ("self-initiated learning," "students pursuing their interests without interruption," phrases appropriated from Sudbury) had camouflaged our differences. We had rallied around concepts that we now enacted in amazingly varied, and eventually opposing, ways. "Initiative" and "interruption" are ideas, interpretations. They exist in the eye of the beholder, not in the external world. They are not real, not in the way that students approaching the door on the first day of school are real. Not in the way that actions are real.

Before the students arrived, I thought everyone at Cascade Valley School shared my values. I thought everyone wanted what I wanted: students building forts, making music, sitting around complaining they had nothing to do. I thought everyone scorned what I scorned: training children to replace their experience with someone else's judgment—teachers enthusing "Good jumping!" while young children jump around like young children naturally do. Or principals determining who "wins" student body elections.

At our school, what to learn would be up to each student. Voting would be real—that is, each student and each member of the staff would have a vote, an equal say, with the majority determining everything from the school's rules to its staff. There was no clearer way to demonstrate that Cascade Valley School trusted its students and believed in their competence. Nor could any curriculum be more demanding.

Preview

The summer before the school opened, I got a glimpse of how I thought Cascade Valley would work:

The doorbell rang and my four-year-old rushed to the door, excited that people were meeting at our house. Then Julia saw someone she didn't expect—another committee member had brought along her daughter, also four years old.

"She can't come in," said my daughter, pushing the door shut. "She can't play with my toys. I don't want Veda in my house. Why is she here?"

"They're here for my meeting," I told her, and opened the door. Julia retreated to her room, insisting the other child stay out.

Both Veda's mother and I took short breaks to comfort our distraught children. Neither of us suggested ways they could solve their dilemma: we hadn't been asked.

That meeting introduced me to the first parent I had ever met whose commitment to treating children as competent equaled my own, a stance I came to characterize as *The Real*. She did not think of her daughter as helpless— she saw her as someone with a problem, a problem the child had the resources to solve. (Eventually Veda asked me if *I* had any toys she could play with. I brought her a stack of my picture books and a wire whisk.)

As the hopeful will, I generalized. I imagined that our committee meeting depicted values held by everyone starting the school. In fact, it described one of two competing dreams that people had for the school.

Two Dreams

Two dreams draw people to the Sudbury model of education. I call one dream and its proponents The Kind, and I call the other dream and its proponents The Real. The contrasting perspectives, minus each side's inflammatory language, boil down to this:

> The Kind want a school where children are happy and involved, where they are treated well—a kind place. They theorize that the school's tolerance and understanding will produce students who behave in tolerant and understanding ways.

> The Real want a school where students can do something about feeling sad or bored or mistreated—something concrete, something real. They theorize that such a school will produce students who can identify what they want and devise ways to get it.

The Kind emphasize students being, or becoming, kind or happy or good. Proponents of this dream focus on aspects of the Sudbury model like "students pursuing their own interests." Self-initiated learning fits The Kind's antiauthoritarian values and meets their prerequisite that students enjoy themselves. As they see it, developing individuals who feel good about themselves (and whose behavior will then serve the greater good) is the school's purpose.

The Real believe in self-initiated learning as well, but their definition focuses on what students learn by struggling with problems that matter to them—the reason I neither forced my daughter to share her toys nor suggested ways the other girl could entertain herself. Proponents of The Real want the school to promote effectiveness, the capacity to move skillfully from wish to idea to follow-through. In line with their beliefs, The Real champion structures that assure students have access to power, structures like the School Meeting, where each student and each member of the staff have a vote. (The School Meeting—pioneered by England's Summerhill and democratized by Sudbury—determines the school's rules and expenditures: whether to mend or replace a broken basketball hoop, whether to expel an unruly student, criteria for using the school's computers, procedures for cleaning the kitchen, and so on.)

The Kind, on the other hand, argue that people of different ages have such different skills that it hardly matters whether everyone is *entitled* to vote at the School Meeting. They see the students as disadvantaged, despite their numerical capacity to outvote the staff. The Kind therefore try to soften outcomes they see as cruel and The Real see as consequences of their actions: outcomes that derive from reality and not from the age or the verbal skill of the miscreant. Students running a snack bar included a sticky-fingered pal in their operation—and lost their money. (In this case, The Real prevailed and the students had to pay, out of pocket, the percentage of the snack bar profits they had promised the School Meeting.) The student who threw a bike in the school's pond got suspended: not for getting angry—that was his business—but for getting close enough to the pond to endanger the school's lease.

Divisions like *The Kind* and *The Real* are artificial, of course, but labeling our differences helps me parse Cascade Valley's tumultuous first year. The Kind and The Real provide an overview, an orientation. I need one. I'm still startled by the year's vehemence, by differences so extreme they split the school. I'm still stunned that a group of people who succeeded, against long odds, in opening a school, ended up drawing a line in the dirt and slugging it out.

Differences

Differences between The Kind and The Real surfaced as soon as the school opened. Interventions that seemed reasonable to The Kind, with their focus on happiness— "redirecting" a bored child, for instance, by suggesting something fun to do—horrified The Real. Boredom is instructive, they insisted: some choices lead to tedium, others to fascination. Disengaged students need time, not rescue: time to discover which choices lead where. Hands off!

But The Real also insisted that members of the staff who withheld their opinions and their School Meeting votes to "see what the students wanted" were patronizing the students. Students would not become more adept, per The Kind's intention, as a result of the adults at the school dumbing down. Besides, they urged, democracy requires everybody's best efforts: a ten-year-old student's best efforts, a forty-year-old staff member's best efforts. The Kind countered that the school's unfamiliar structure overwhelmed students; unless adults took a back seat, students would not speak. Over and over, the staff debated the difference between responsiveness and rescue, between clarity and rigidity—debates that did more to develop positions than to resolve questions.

Parents did more than debate. The Kind among them attacked the hands-off members of the staff, those who most treasured students working things out for themselves. Why, such parents demanded, were certain members of the staff ignoring children who needed their help? Should a school even expose children to people like that, people who don't care about children? One parent made the Orwellian suggestion that we require attendance at School Meeting— "so students will realize they're free to decide what goes on at the school."

More than philosophy was at stake. The amount of adult intervention advocated by The Kind was anathema to those who most valued student initiative. The Real's belief that unhappy students would, eventually, do something about their discontent required The Kind to tolerate levels of distress they considered inhumane. Neither side, in good conscience, could go along with the other. From the day it first opened, September 7, 1991, Cascade Valley School was on a collision course.

Factions

People on both sides hoped the school could find a middle ground. People on both sides hoped we were fighting about tone and not content:

> The Kind thought those on the other side talked tougher than was called for, "but maybe that's how they sound under stress"—a kindly assumption.

> The Real questioned whether they weren't being too hard on their counterparts. "It's not as though we know how to implement these unfamiliar ideas any better"—a realistic consideration.

We could have used two columns, one labeled *Kind*, and the other, *Real*, to tally most first-year votes. We debated everything from these competing perspectives—hours, salaries, scholarships, the authority of the School Meeting itself. Like the oil and vinegar in a homemade vinaigrette, our positions separated out over time, becoming distinct and visible.

Even if the entire group had been of one mind, we would still have had problems. The line between freedom and license is hard to find. Finding it while learning a new paradigm is even harder. Adding to the difficulties inherent in starting a school was the dominant culture's tendency to either indulge children or control them, a tendency illustrated by free schools at one extreme and military schools at the other. We wanted a third option, neither indulgent nor controlling: a school where students had genuine choice and with it, genuine responsibility.

We frequently slid past it. We did what beginners do, lurched our way toward consistency:

"When students mess up, there should be repercussions."

"No, not 'repercussions.' There should be 'learning experiences.'"

"Wait a minute, the entire incident is none of our business."

"The minute something affects the rest of the school, it *becomes* our business."

Staff meetings looked like tennis matches, with heads (and positions) swiveling from side to side. Everyone took a while to find the target zone. This was highlighted by the message another member of the first year staff left on my home answering machine:

"Driving home, I understood why you got so annoyed with the position I took in today's School Meeting. You were right. I should have confronted the students involved. Thanks." My face flushed as I listened. She had left me the message I had intended to leave her the week before, when we had landed on opposite sides of a different issue. On the way home, I had realized that *she* was right.

Flip-flopping between positions is typical of beginners. It takes a long time to practice any methodology consistently or well, and even longer to feel it in your bones. Starting a democratic school is a doozie of a training program, the steepest learning curve I know. (It took me, for instance, seven months to get clear about the responsibilities of the School Meeting, and even then I needed confirmation—data that I later used to reassure bewildered newcomers.) None of us had grown up with what we wanted our students to have. We had to create a democratic school inside ourselves as well as externally: in conversations with students, with parents, with one another. In the office, in the cubby room, beside the pond.

It took us the better part of a year. It took that long to begin to distinguish between supporting students and indulging them, to recognize the difference between predictability and inflexibility. Not that we were skilled, but we had begun to think in ways we did not—and could not—think in September, when we opened the school.

Mistakes

Cascade Valley School made an impressive number of mistakes its first year. We recovered from enough of them that the school is still standing. One mistake that will have consequences past the year 2000 was the assumption that our first-year enrollment would top 32 students. All our finances were based on that goal, one we didn't meet until our fourth year. As a result, we're considerably in the hole. It's a mistake I find endearing, a memento of the ignorant enthusiasm it takes to start a school. We fully expected parents to flock to the school, eager to enroll their children. After all, we were in love with the idea, we were turning our lives inside out to start a radical, democratic, initiative-based school.

My dismay over the battles of our first year has receded. So has the chagrin I feel about some of my contributions to them. What I feel instead is calm conviction. Starting a school is so sizable a task, and democratic values so little practiced, that no Sudbury-inspired group could possibly stay out of trouble. Maybe no group with democratic ambitions can, whether the group is the local food co-op or the U.S. Senate.

Happiness

Some adults seem drawn to democratic schooling by visions of kindly, contented, justice-loving children. As soon as our first-year students found meetings boring, elections difficult, or the school's requirements demanding, The Kind got frantic. In their version of a well-run school, nothing would make anyone unhappy. Unhappiness proved something was wrong. The clearer their position came, the greater my amazement. I thought democracy assured everyone's *occasional* unhappiness—its virtue lay in spreading it around.

I thought the purpose of the school's Judicial Committee (the branch of the School Meeting in charge of discipline) was, in a sense, unhappiness. The JC had the job of communicating the larger group's unhappiness with certain behaviors. It had the job of protecting individual rights while upholding the school's rules—partly by figuring out, case by case, what would make rule-breakers unhappy enough to change their behavior.

Sentenced to replace the 35-cent pencils they had appropriated, two of our younger students "forgot" to satisfy their sentence for days on end. They made new excuses daily: they didn't have their allowances, their mothers hadn't taken them to the store. The Judicial Committee extended the date for completing their sentence, and again they delayed, coming up with still more excuses. The JC discussed their non-compliance, and someone proposed yet another extension.

Then one of those serving on the JC (a preteen who had himself resisted JC's authority when he first came to the school) exclaimed, "Wait a minute! They're ignoring us and that's not right. Let's come up with a sentence that matters to them." So the Judicial Committee excluded the students from the sandbox until they replaced the pencils, which they did that very afternoon.

Those testing how much they can get away with are engaged in important learning; so are those—3 or 4 students and a member of the staff—whose job it is to hold the line.

Politics

Proponents of The Kind elected students to school offices because "they need the experience," not because they would get the job done. The Kind seemed to find politics distasteful and politicking contemptible, whereas The Real—well, The Real thought politicking got things done. When The Real voted to suspend students for conduct they thought jeopardized the school, The Kind worried that the students would then view the school as "uncaring."

Proponents of The Real expected people of all ages to learn from their mistakes, lobby for what they wanted, then go along with what the majority decided. Students who argued that the Judicial Committee should not charge them with violating a rule, for example, generally pleaded "guilty" if they were charged anyway. The majority had spoken.

One of the school's founders remained calm while the group passed proposals he utterly opposed. He thought sorry outcomes would follow, but he also thought that the outcomes he predicted would change future votes. Either that, or he'd discover that his predictions were off. The Real's commitment was to a specific way of doing things —democratic governance, majority rule—and not to the results of a given vote or to a psychological outcome like "happiness" or "empowerment" or "harmony."

Assessment

The Real supported initiative-based learning because they had never seen anything else work. They told stories about no longer remembering facts they had been forced to learn, and still remembering ones they had sought out. For The Real, students who complained of boredom were detoxifying, recovering from years of force-feeding. Next they would figure out what interested them; eventually they would do something about it. The same way that members of the staff, equally new to democratic schooling, would eventually discover how to do their jobs.

It took everyone a long time to realize that those assessing the school were coming up with different evaluations because they—we—were using different criteria. And different memories: The Kind's schooling stories focused on subjects they didn't value at the time, but now were now glad that someone had insisted they learn.

The Kind saw suffering where others saw struggle. They then invented schemes to entertain students they thought were bored, arguing that before students could make choices, they had to "be exposed to what's out there." Doubtful that student inertia would recede, they demanded proof that it had. In the meantime, they argued, staff should keep students occupied.

Over time, it became apparent that The Kind and The Real used words like "initiative" and "self-selection" to mean different things. One mother screamed that the school's staff had refused to teach her six-year-old to read. The staff thought the boy had plenty of moxie. He had asked for our help with other projects. Since he hadn't asked anyone on the staff to help him learn to read, we figured that reading was the mother's agenda. She thought the staff was tangled in derivative theory, and short on simple common sense. After all, whenever she asked her son, "Don't you want to learn to read?" the boy always answered, "Yes."

The mother's reasoning struck me as goofy at the time. Now the staff's reasoning seems equally suspect. After all, the boy could have been learning to read on his own, or from other students. The reasoning on both sides illustrates the power of cultural assumptions, especially those so widely held that they are rarely named, like "children learn to read from adults." Although Sudbury's literature specifically states that few of their students have ever used adult assistance in learning to read, our habits of mind had not yet shifted. More importantly, we did not know that they had not yet shifted.

This phenomenon underlies my wariness when people with brief exposure to the Sudbury model—a couple of years, say—want to "improve" on it. Ideas that are out of the ordinary take a long time to understand, and even longer to apply intelligently. I therefore assume that would-be reformers are trying to make the Sudbury model familiar, more compatible with their personal values and/or the values of the larger culture. I also assume that such reformers do not recognize that familiarity is what motivates them.

Those of us who spent the year holding the line, insisting that the school do things the ways they're done at Sudbury, did not claim that using Sudbury's methods would assure literacy, for example. We simply held that other methods—whatever their claims—wouldn't either. The Real are pragmatists. Our passion, then and now, was not for students acquiring specific skills. Our passion was for students running their lives.

Accusations

What The Real lacked in rhetoric they made up in obstinance, repeatedly insisting that some principles were central to the school and not to be tinkered with. Charges that they were inflexible or "just copying Sudbury" did not shake them, although accusations that they were damaging children did.

Some of the bruises each faction inflicted on the other came from the crucially different ways they evaluated the school. The Kind saw children who were happy, or not, and used that assessment to form their opinions. They were for the procedures and people they believed made children happy; they were against those they believed made children unhappy. For them, what to do was clear and the time for change long past. The Real saw things differently. They saw vibrant children—sometimes happy and sometimes unhappy—who were doing well despite the school's first-year fumbles.

The Kind and The Real handled their concerns in diametrically different ways. When The Kind perceived that something was wrong, they urged change, the sooner the better. The Real responded to similar situations by taking a deep breath and trying to do, more skillfully, what they had been doing all along. They believed that applying Sudbury's procedures (even if ineptly) would prove, at a future date, to have been the right thing to do.

The Real had no interest in starting a school per se, only in starting a school like Sudbury Valley School. And for them, it was too soon to tell whether Cascade Valley would succeed.

Anxiety

People who found resistance where they had expected cooperation and experienced anxiety where they had expected contentment were understandably upset. Worse, they felt tricked. The Kind had anticipated a school where happy children achieved conventional goals without coercion. That's what they'd signed on for. "My child isn't learning to read (apprenticing somewhere exciting, going on enough field trips)," fumed parents in this camp, "and you don't even care!" Their expectations had been thwarted, and they were too upset to consider the possibility that their expectations—and not the school—needed to change.

They had no patience for theories that children who spent as much time as they wanted building forts in the blackberry bushes, the year's favorite activity, were increasing their capacity to focus, a capacity that would serve them whatever they decided to learn next. How to read, for instance. What The Kind saw (kids spending all their time playing, staff refusing to require even a single course) upset them.

The Real had their bad moments too—the first year was hard on all the adults involved—but they tended to read anxiety, including their own, as a sign the school was on track. Allowing young people to take charge of their lives spooks most people. So does choice, if the choices include students "wasting time" or getting into trouble. "Anxiety," pleaded The Real, "is the cost of living outside generally-held assumptions. For the school's offer of freedom to be genuine, we have to tolerate our own discomfort."

"Discomfort is supposed to spur change. Greenberg says so right here," countered parents who believed that their distress signaled general wrack and ruin. Since they were uncomfortable, the school should change. People like me, reading the same literature, had envisioned student discomfort motivating *students* to change. It was the "divided by a common language" issue yet again. Each reader had pictured a school that fit that reader's history and politics and parenting practices, which is the danger of starting a school from books.

Anxiety fills the gap between what people imagine will happen and what actually happens. Reading Greenberg, people got the idea that students at Sudbury are busy all the time. Students at Sudbury *are* busy all the time, but they are busy doing whatever interests them: playing guitar, dozing in the sun, turning cartwheels, hanging out. Greenberg describes them as busy because, in his eyes, they are. He describes them as learning prodigiously for the same reason.

The parents who had read Greenberg or attended one of our Open Houses formed more conventional images. If science was their Johnny's favorite subject, they pictured Johnny spending all his time at Cascade Valley doing science. They formed images that assumed limited alternatives: science *or* English, reading *or* math. But at Cascade Valley School, Johnny had a different set of alternatives. He could wander off by himself if he felt like it. Read to a little kid. Organize a game of tag or a change in the school's rules. He could pursue whatever interested him, including topics generally thought of as science.

When the school didn't match people's internal images— images that none of us knew were images but believed were goals we had in common—we became anxious.

"Why not post a list of the classes that staff members know how to teach? Then students would know what's available."

"Don't you see? A list like that would define learning as something that teachers organize; it would label specific activities as the useful ones."

Something was wrong, our nervous systems thrummed. Wrong! Unaware that part of what felt so wrong came from inside us, we looked to our surroundings. Something was wrong out there—wrong with the school, wrong with the model, wrong with the people on the other side. Specific things *were* wrong, of course: Cascade Valley School was a start-up operation. But much of everyone's distress, I now believe, came from the difference between what people expected and what they got.

Only the hopeful start schools. We were all hopeful, the parents who had enrolled their children, the students themselves, those who signed on as first-year staff. We had promised ourselves a wonderful new school—forgetting that voracious anxiety accompanies anything new. Some who came to Cascade Valley School delighted by the idea that students would chose their own activities, couldn't handle the rest of the package: votes that didn't go the way they thought they should go, students not getting what they wanted on the first try. They had signed on for kind and happy.

Lifetime Applicability

I had signed on for Sudbury's tough-mindedness, for its emphasis on students' rights and its equal emphasis on their responsibilities. I had signed on for adults who respected play, who appreciated independence, who didn't need to be needed. I had signed on for annually elected staff in place of tenured teachers and entrenched bureaucracies. At last, education reform that amounted to something.

It wasn't that I had some perverse attachment to difficulty for its own sake. I just couldn't see much difference between what others claimed were Good Schools and Bad Schools. True, conventional schools were meaninglessly rigid but progressive schools were just as meaninglessly flexible. In neither case could students use the schools as practice for the rest of their lives. Adults don't have to raise their hands to go the bathroom, as Bad Schools force their students to do. But neither are they coaxed into playing nicely or given stickers for following the rules, as students are in schools that call themselves Good.

For me, the hope that Cascade Valley School would guarantee my four-year-old a childhood was sufficient reason to start a school. She would have a haven, protected

from the "more is better and earliest is best" thinking that
dominates contemporary education. She would have a variety of people, including adults, to study. She would learn
that rules are to be obeyed *and* rules are to be changed, that
individuals have rights *and* so do groups. That is, she would
learn the perspective and skills an American citizen needs.

The First Year

I had expected students to be on edge most of the first
year, incredulous they had so much freedom, worried there
was some catch. I had expected adults to sympathize while
holding the line. Wrong. Most students quickly found ways
to feel comfortable. Four and five-year-olds who began
their school careers at Cascade Valley were busy and happy
from the beginning. School-savvy older students manipu-
lated as many of the staff as were manipulatable and looked
after themselves the rest of the time. Even the students who
daily pleaded for rides to the deli seemed okay with "Are
you kidding?" as the standard reply. They were sounding
out the staff as much as finagling a ride.

The adults, on the other hand, lost it.

Staff and parents had—and caused—far more trouble
than students. Adults of the kindliness persuasion raged
when their discontent didn't spur reform. I raged too. We
had agreed, I kept insisting, we had agreed—on philosophy,
on procedure.

The Real mistook their passions for the group's desires.
The Kind mistook their anxieties for the school's deficien-
cies. Everyone felt betrayed. Each faction had imagined
that everyone supported whichever was their version of
the school: The Kind, The Real. Each tried to convince

the other. Each found their own data compelling and their own suggestions sensible.

"Students are suffering," declared The Kind. "They need more structure, more encouragement, more opportunities."

"Students are struggling," countered The Real. "They need more time, more trust, fewer interruptions."

Conflict dominated Cascade Valley School's first year. Not only did the two versions of the school differ (each, of course, claiming Sudbury-derived authority), neither side felt it could live with what the other wanted. Finally, the faction I've called The Kind withdrew their children, reducing the school's enrollment by a third. The school clicked into place the next day. Students whose parents believed they required constant supervision (and whose behavior proved the point) were gone. What remained, by and large, were students who had been reared to behave responsibly.

Second Ascent

The year was brutal—I have never been through anything like it. But then, I had a long way to fall. I thought I had found a group of adults whose passion for democratic education and self-initiated learning matched my own. The fact is, people ran for staff because they needed a job. The fact is, parents enrolled their children because the school they preferred had a waiting list or charged higher tuition.

I kept notes from the very beginning, hoping to help others start Sudbury-inspired schools. I pictured a how-to book, with chapters on PR, on fund-raising, on hiring first-year staff. I played with *Second Ascent* as a title. Second ascent is the mountaineering term for climbing a mountain that's been scaled once before. Second ascents are easier, experienced climbers say, because you know the mountain can be climbed. As our first year got harder and meaner, my hopes for the book constricted until all that remained was the title. Then a book entitled *Second Ascent* came out. Its author, a man mutilated in a climbing accident, kept trying to scale world-class mountains with what remained of his arms and legs.

"That pretty much describes us and what we're trying to do," I muttered, mouth set in a grim line.

This, six months after we opened—this is how embattled I felt. This is how hard it is to start a school. How hard it is, at any rate, for people with hopes and illusions. And who but the hopeful ever start anything?

Long Distance

Phone conversations with Sudbury's founders helped me survive Cascade Valley's contentious first year. The day after the school split, I telephoned my mentors. I told them that I had always assumed that starting a school would be hard. "But if you had tried to tell me how hard, I wouldn't have believed you." I simply did not know that anything got this hard. Luckily, my positive expectations were off, too. "Everything," I told them, "everything about the school, both good and bad, has been far more intense than anything I could have imagined."

They knew what I meant, they told me. That was how they had spent the past twenty-some years.

"You mean," I squeaked, "it's always like this? This combination of worse-than-I-could-have-imagined and better-than-I-could-have-hoped and sometimes I'm wrong and sometimes the other person's wrong but after a while it doesn't matter and you keep going because the school has to be there for your child?"

They started to laugh. "We knew you had no idea what you were getting yourself into. But we didn't think you would have understood, even if we had tried to tell you."

Could they have told me? Would I have understood? What if they had warned me that concerns about kindness frequently mask condescending views of children? What if they had predicted that I was so accustomed to adult privilege that I wouldn't know how to proceed in its absence? What if they had cautioned me that few of the people who claim to support a radical concept have the conviction it takes to follow through? What if they had warned me: once parents see what student choice looks like in operation, all hell will break lose.

Would their admonitions have alarmed me?

Absolutely. Would they have stopped me? I hope not.

Looking Back

Five years later, Cascade Valley School is still standing. Other schools, started at the same time, are not. I am in charge of admissions. Students trying to decide whether to enroll juggle questions that have only subjective answers. Will taking responsibility for themselves prove harder than following directions? Will they enjoy themselves?

If they ask me, I tell them what my introduction to the school was like. It was hard, I tell them, hard in ways I hadn't expected. And yes, I enjoy the school—also in ways I hadn't expected. None of my fantasies about the school, fantasies so powerful they compelled me to join with others to start a school, prepared me for the joy I felt when:

A parent I barely knew stopped me in the parking lot to encourage me to "hang in there" while people attacked my vision of the school—and offered to coach me so I could.

A girl I tutored asked me for extra classes and harder homework, just like students do in Greenberg's books.

A boy went outside and ran around the building to get sufficient command of himself to make it through the School Meeting where students and staff, in tears, voted to expel him.

But the image that stays with me is this one: students rushing outside to dance on the school lawn in the first hard rain. The rain, mixed with hail, came down at a slant. It looked like the drawings of rain in children's books, hitting the ground so hard it bounced back up.

First a few of the older boys, then several girls, then a mix of the younger students ran out into the rain, to whirl and slide and dance. Looking up, getting soaked, they laughed as the rain pelted them. Palms to the sky like Balinese dancers, the students paused to catch hailstones, then went back to twirling. Dancing.

Then and there, I stopped weighing the hardships of our first year. I was where I wanted to be, on the porch at Cascade Valley School, giddy, exhausted, and grateful for my good fortune. Five years later, I finally understand why the image stays with me: you get drenched starting a school. Pelted. Stung. But the rain that comes down harder than you ever thought rain could come down, bounces back up. Extend your hands. Dance.

Appendix 4

Revolution or Reform?
Thoughts on the Character, Strategy and Destiny of Sudbury Valley School

Daniel Greenberg (1971)

I

We have many problems we are trying to cope with in the school now, and I feel that they are all part of a single theme; problems like how we are going to increase our enrollment, what our relationship ought to be to schools and organizations, how we should conduct our publicity campaign, what (if anything) we should do to increase the school's utilization of the staff, how we should deal with visitors. All these are open questions now, because we've never really settled them. In past years, we have dealt with them mostly by gut intuition. Now, suddenly, we feel in need of a policy, partly because there are just too many of them to handle without guidelines, and partly because I think we want to get our identity a little clearer.

All the pieces fit together for me now, for the first time. The key has been the realization that we have had two distinct characters existing in parallel from the time the school was in its earliest planning stages—two characters that are basically incompatible, and whose conflict has created a lot of tension (much of it good for the school) and made it difficult to get a clear picture of what the school is. Although, in retrospect, I don't know that it could have been different.

The two characters that have coexisted in us during these years are a reformist character and a revolutionary character. Let me just say a word about how I understand each of these concepts. To reform something means to make changes in its present structure, but in a way that is sympathetic to the fundamental concepts underlying the structure. You really like the structure you are reforming, you like what it is, but there are certain flaws in it that you've noticed, either because it isn't operating the way it was supposed to, or because you don't quite like the way it was supposed to. By contrast, to revolutionize something means to redo entirely its fundamental aspects, because you have found it to be basically unsatisfactory and you want to reconstruct it from scratch.

There is a common misconception that the difference between reform and revolutionize has to do with the means. In fact, it has nothing at all to do with the means. It has to do with the basic assumptions. The assumption of reform is that what you're reforming is, at the heart of it, healthy and only needs a little doctoring. A lot of things follow from that: for example, the tactics of reform. You don't want to upset the apple cart. On the contrary, you want people to accept you, because you are basically in sympathy with what they are doing, you are basically in tune with them. So you don't want to make enemies. The last thing that a reformer wants to do is make enemies. A reformer wants to love everybody, and he wants everybody to love him. More than that, he wants everybody to cooperate with him, because he is close to them at heart. Reformers have a fundamentally friendly and cooperative attitude.

Another consequence of the nature of reform is the length of time involved in the process. Reform is a shorter-cycled process relative to revolution, because it is not as fundamental, it doesn't strike at the roots of existence. Because of this, it can't hold people's commitment very long; it's more like a surface perturbation, and either it takes or it doesn't take in a short period of time. Again, once it does take, the standard thing happens that one hears so much about: the reformers then become integrated into the Establishment, because that is in fact how they were basically all along.

Revolutionary tactics are almost the opposite. Revolutionaries know that because they are seeking to overturn some very basic features of the institution they are attacking, they cannot expect most of the people involved in that institution to embrace them. Such an expectation would just be folly, because most of those people are committed to the basic world-view being challenged by the revolution. So revolutionaries know that they cannot expect cooperation from a lot of people. As a result, revolutionary tactics have to be centered on building a strong enough advanced guard to carry out the revolution—strong enough and determined enough to overcome the entrenched interests that they are trying to overthrow. Generally, theirs is a more aggressive policy, mainly because they seek to uproot something, also because they have to separate the sheep from the goats very quickly, in order to find the people who are really committed and willing to go through with it.

What goes with that is the span of time that is involved. You get people in a revolution who are much more committed, because the change they seek is much deeper, and once they have made the commitment to that change there is no turning back. As a result, they can maintain their commitment over long periods of time. You can think of a revolution as taking on the order of a generation, because—as Max Planck said for physics, and as he might have said for everything else—basically, in order to carry out a revolution, you have got to wait until the whole generation dies, since the generation in which the revolution started is committed to its own world-view. So you must build a revolutionary cadre, and you maybe even succeed to a certain extent, step by step, to spread your program; but you carry it through only in a generation's time, only when you have a whole new generation that can break out of old patterns.

With these general comments as background, we can ask now in a way that I don't think we could when we started: is the school's philosophy revolutionary or reformist? What is the strategy appropriate to it? Never mind for a moment what we have done in the past, let's just look at it now and ask, what is its character? What are the things it stands for? Then we can trace back and set the present in perspective.

I think that now we can pinpoint the things we really stand for. Very sharply. As I see it, they are two. First, we are very much oriented towards each person going as far as he can towards his own internally self-consistent destiny. We stand for the fullest possible realization of individual potential. We start with the individual. For us, actions of the community as a whole are something necessary—they have to happen, and we set up mechanisms to enable them to happen—but only as a last resort.

For example, that's how we determine when we need formal, communally controlled administration in the school. We start with every area of administration in individual hands—it's just typical of the whole philosophy of the school. And we let it go as far as we can until problems start developing. It's only when a certain critical mass of problems has been reached, so large that we no longer feel we can tolerate them, that we intrude a communal administrative apparatus. The same thing happens with the judicial system, and with everything else.

That's the fundamental philosophical world-view. We don't elevate the community, the nation, the race, the school, the family, or whatever; we start with the individual, and all of the other trappings are brought in to the minimum extent possible, as sort of necessary evils. This world-view has many ramifications and implications. Because of it, we protect individual rights zealously. After all, individual rights are not so important to other groups. In our case, it is our bias toward the individual that stands out. The same holds for the concept of each person learning what he wants to learn, each person thinking what he wants to think, and all these things that we stress over and over again—each person being responsible for his behavior, for his education. Extreme individualism. Of course, we have exceptions. We say that each person is responsible for his own fate in the school, but we have had to yield a little—it's not as if we are dogmatic purists in these matters. But it takes an awful lot of persuasion to convince anybody in the school, in any area, that you have to take communal action in regard to an individual. It's always, "If you want to find out something, go to the files." Even the concept of the School Meeting Record is something that was long in coming: "If you want to know what the motions are that we're going to vote on, come to the School Meeting and remember them, or write them down." Slowly, we pulled back from that position, and made the great concession of publishing the School Meeting Record. But basically our orientation was that each person had to take care of his own interests in the School Meeting, and if he didn't, it was too bad for him. So, many consequences flow from this position; it's very central to the school.

The other central conception to the school is that community action is taken through as pure a democracy as one can possibly put together. Everybody affected by every communal activity has a right to have a full say in determining it. In a sense, the one person-one vote idea is itself a consequence of the elevation of the individual; but the idea of the democratic political process is a separate idea, and has its own place in our philosophy.

If you accept this capsule summary of what the school stands for, then the question is, "Are these conceptions revolutionary or reformist in the context of society at large?" Now, I don't think that when we started we focussed as sharply as we do now on the basic aspects of the school. I think if you go back to our literature you will indeed find these themes very clearly; they are not missing. But I don't think it was that focussed. I think it was mixed with other concepts of educational reform. In other words, there were a lot of concepts floating around, and they were all given equal priority; there was no sorting out. If you would have said, when we started, when we wrote our first brochure, "Well now, what does it really boil down to?" we couldn't have answered. The first breakdown in that respect was the third edition of the catalog, where a new section entered that became our theme song: "Responsibility is the key concept of the school." That was the first time when we picked from among all of the ten or fifteen concepts that we would list, one that was kind of primary. If we had to write it over today, we wouldn't even say that. But that was the first step toward distilling the essence. We can go further now, we can be clearer. The essence isn't even "responsibility." The essence is: *respect for individual.* The sacredness of each individual person.

That's the central concept. A step towards that was our setting apart the concept of responsibility; you can see this now, in retrospect. But before we set that apart, in our early literature, we had a whole parallel series of concepts, without any relative weights. So if you would have asked, "Are we reformers or revolutionaries?"—and you wouldn't even have asked that question at the time, because it was too early—but if you would have asked, early in our history we really wouldn't have known how to answer, because we were throwing around so many concepts, some of which were reformist and some of which were revolutionary.

Which brings me to something else I want to say about reform and revolution. Two key features of reform (because it's a corrective mechanism) are *additivity* and *compromisability.* Most reform movements have a series of things they want to correct. They look around, see the flaws, list them, and want to correct them all. In almost every reformist platform you read, "We want this, and we want this, and we want this." This program is additive. And if one or two of the demands are met, then the reformers usually say, "We've taken a couple of steps toward reform." The idea of progress towards the whole program is something characteristic of reform. Also, compromise. Reformers present the list of corrections they want, and then the Establishment will come and say, "You know, you really have a point there. Unfortunately, we can't do it right away, but we'll take our first step toward it"—so the reformer compromises, and says, "Ok, you go half way toward it. Maybe in ten years you can take the next step." Now, these two features of additivity and compromise are meaningless to revolution. Because the essential feature of revolution is the whole gestalt. There's a whole new world-view being advocated and it all fits together. The pieces don't hang separately; you either have to take in the whole picture or you're missing the point.

Even in our very first "About," when we listed the "key features of the school" and came up with some ten, we felt that we were doing something not quite right; so we added a whole page saying, in effect, "Don't think these are just ten additive features; they are all interrelated and they form a consistent whole." You could see the struggle between the two tendencies even there. Of course, somebody reading the "About" would more likely than not consider us a reformist movement with a ten point platform, and would ignore the last page. We ourselves weren't sure of our stance, but we realized that it wasn't simply reform, because we did add that last page. Also, we have always been called uncompromising. For us, as far as our basic premises go, compromise is a meaningless concept. You can't compromise respect for a human being. Other things, maybe. Freedom, for example is highly relative, and is always compromised to some extent. But freedom isn't the key to our school. It's not just a question of freedom. It's a question of basic respect for a person.

We stand for a whole way of life, a life style that is not a simple small perturbation of the surrounding. This relates to our book, "The Crisis in American Education." In order to be revolutionary, you don't have to be new. A revolutionary movement is not necessarily, or even usually, a movement that creates brand new concepts that were never on the scene before. The only criterion for revolution versus reform is whether or not it's different from the basic conceptions that are *current* in the surrounding culture. The Reformation did not create new concepts; it revived the old ones that were very much part of the early Church. The American Revolution did didn't create new concepts. To be sure, sometimes you get new concepts; but that's not a necessity. The point is that at the time of the revolution, it is in conflict with the surrounding culture. That, I think, is the real lesson the "Crisis" book has brought home. That book tries to point out the degree to which our school's conceptions are part of the American heritage; the book purposely glosses over the degree to which these fundamental conceptions of the American heritage are out of tune with the way American is today. That glossing over is what infuriates the liberals and the reformers more than anything else. When they read the book, they cry out, "How can you say that America believes in equal opportunity when this and this and this isn't the case? How can you say that there is democracy? Etc. Etc." Their reaction demonstrates the point I am making: our principles, even though they are part of the American heritage, are out of tune with the American culture today. And that is why these people get upset. What they see is the present ambience, and our basic principles are not the basic principles of the present American scene. They are basic to the American heritage, but they are not the underlying conceptions of the present American culture. So that the reformers who get our book feel that it is a misrepresentation; they realize that it is really a revolutionary book. It can only really appeal to people who are ready to make a leap out of the present cultural setting back to the roots of the American experience.

The question of whether revolutionary concepts are new or not is very strongly related to the degree to which they are likely to succeed. I think that if you are lucky enough in a revolution to be dealing in a world-view that does have roots in the culture in which your revolution is taking place, then you are more likely to succeed. But if your revolution has to create from scratch the conceptions at its base, it's going to have a harder time taking root. I would image that if you looked at the history of revolutions, the ones that took longest are the ones that were farthest from the heritage of the culture in which they took place. Christianity in the Roman world took generations. The Reformation happened almost overnight, because it resonated with vibrations that were present in Europe at the time. I guess the real thing to study is revolutionary attempts that failed; but there is very little record of most of them because the victors usually expunge most of it from the history books.

There is another point worth touching on—the question of whether or not a revolution must be violent, because it takes place at such a basic level. Most people think of a revolution as being violent. I think it is of necessity violent, except that the word "violent" has to be given a broader interpretation than simply a resort to arms. A revolution must involve extremes of emotion and extremes of commitment. The people who are trying to carry it out have to be dogged, stubborn, and firm; they must possess a rock-like strength that is brutally determined, and they must expect to face opposition that is murderously strong in return. You can point to revolutions that didn't lead to wars, but they all involved, at the very least, immense emotional upheavals. The Christian revolution is a good example. The scientific revolution, the industrial revolution—these were carried out by men having a very strong will. There was some bloodletting in many of these, because of the violent nature of the societies in which they took place. But they didn't involve wars, like the French Revolution, or the American Revolution, or the Russian Revolution, and they weren't really warlike.

We at the school have probably got to accept the face that what we are doing is not reformist, but revolutionary. The kinds of things we stand for are simply not small modifications of the surrounding culture, but big ones: the sacredness of the individual, regardless of age, sex, color, anything—the idea that every human being should a priori be allowed full expression of his character; and the idea that the extent to which the community infringes on a person's independence must be decided by as pure a democracy as possible—with all that is attendant on this idea, like complete openness, and honesty, and candor, and frankness, and representation, and accessibility. These are the underpinnings of the life style that we talk about, and all the educational work, all the communal work, all the juridical work, and everything else in the school draws on these two concepts. And they are *not* minor modifications of the surrounding culture. They are rooted in the American tradition, but they are not small perturbations of the current American scene. So in today's America, our kind of enterprise is revolutionary. More that than: it is unlike any other revolutionary movement underway in America today. I think once you pinpoint what it is we stand for, you can see how unlike any other group we really are. For example, compared to the New Left, which speaks so much of participatory democracy, you can see immediately that we are at the other end of the spectrum from them. The New Left begins with the sacredness of the community rather than of the individual. I happen to think that they are reformists; because I think that if anything the tendency in this country is toward elevation of the community at the expense of the individual. As this country departed from its individualistic origins, as it abandoned such policies as open immigration, pluralism in social structures and in cultures, as it came to insist on being a melting pot, and introduced such features as universal education and universal indoctrination, this country has become more and more focussed on nationalism, on common denominators, on federalism, on centralism, and generally on the supremacy of the commonality. You can see a real trend in this country's history from pluralism and individualism and pure democracy towards community control and de-emphasis of the individual and deflation of individual worth. And the New Left simply takes this trend a bit further. It is a reformist movement, and has all the trappings of a reformist movement: the quick fads that go with it, the short cycles, the mass support on a superficial level; and constantly the attempt to coopt. They will take anybody and coopt him; they'll form alliances right and left for any short term advantage, since they are not in danger of compromising a revolutionary core philosophy which they don't have. It fits the fact that so many of them are intellectuals; intellectuals are students of the culture, and are devoted to the culture and to its continued promulgation.

II

If we review the history of every single aspect of the school, we will see the reformist and revolutionary tendencies vying with each other from the very beginning. Consider, again, our educational program. We pursued a whole line of publicity (and activity) that presented us as a reforming institution among educational institutions. For example, as I mentioned earlier, we listed our educational features: we didn't have fixed classes, we waited for self-motivation to take place, etc.—we used a whole set of themes and slogans that were familiar to the educational community, were being bandied around, but were nevertheless beyond what they were doing at the moment. That's on the one hand. When we went somewhere to speak, and to present our educational program, we would so often have a pleading side: "Look, fellas, we're doing the kinds of things you would really believe in, if you only looked." And of course, in response, people would come in from the free school movement, or from regular schools, and say, "Well, we've been doing this particular thing. Don't you think we have gone a long way toward implementing your educational program? Isn't our school really a lot like Sudbury Valley now that we allow so much individual choice of courses?" As I recall it was only about a year or so ago that we started realizing that there is a deeper principle involved in what we are doing. I remember how some of us first started using the words: "There's a moral principle involved. For example, even if the learning process at Sudbury Valley *wasn't* more effective, ours is still the *right* way to conduct a school. Even if our students didn't reach higher achievement levels, what we are doing stands on its own, and has nothing to do with all these other reformist approaches that are based on current educational principles." So ultimately we realized that our educational message was revolutionary: we don't care what the current norms are; the whole point of present-day education is not of interest to us. We do not feel institutionally responsible for conveying a certain body of knowledge, or body of attitudes, to the younger generation. That's revolutionary. And that's *really* what we were saying all along, from the beginning. And once you've said that, all the rest follows: you don't have classes, you don't have evaluations, etc. Individually, other schools can have any one of these specific features, but as long as they still feel committed to getting across a certain amount of subject matter, or a certain set of attitudes, they are miles apart from us.

To be sure, we are certainly committed to a definite system of values. That's what we started with. But we are not committed to transmitting it. We don't feel responsible for seeing to it that our students absorb and accept our values, in the sense that a standard educational institution is committed to teaching. Nor do we have any of the trappings of teaching. We don't have any method for evaluating a student's progress toward becoming independent. We assume his independence; but we don't feel obligated to make *him* accept his independence. Of course it's teaching in the sense that we provide a total value-laden ambience, but it's different from teaching as this is understood in education today—it has nothing in common with schooling.

Take our attitude toward the admissions process. In the early years, there were times when we would have an interview with somebody and the person would storm out, and there were other times when everything was sugar and cake. Any one of us at any given time could have had very different stances towards interviewing enrollees. On the one hand we would try to present the school as an institution that's really compatible with any previous background. The whole question of compatibility was treated lightly. We felt that as long as we said what we were, as long as we didn't try to hide what we were doing, it was a straightforward matter for anybody to enroll. Anybody could fit in, if they wanted to. But there were other times when we would have an interview and really give it to the parents. We would say, "If you don't have respect for your kids, if you don't let them do this and that, you can't even think of sending them."

The question of whether we admit it or just enroll is the same kind of question. I think that our present enrollment policy, that we enroll anybody who wants to come, is a reformist idea. This whole area is very interesting, and very complex. During the first year, we had an *admissions* policy, yet we admitted everybody. You see, even right there we were steeped in ambiguity. We *called* the process admissions; in so doing we were introducing the concept of ideological purity, which is so necessary to revolutionary enterprises. It's a filtration process. And yet from the beginning we applied it in a reformist manner—openly—the assumption being that basically everybody is "OK," and that therefore anybody who would want to would come. Because it's based on the premise that you're not really doing anything very different from what the society at large is doing and therefore anybody can integrate rather nicely. Whereas actually, as we are finding out—and the best proof is the failure of the enrollment to soar dramatically—the difference between what we are doing and the society at large is so great that only a tiny number of people can make the transition.

By now we've gotten completely rid of the side that's compatible with revolutionary movements in our formal procedure; we just enroll. But when we implement the procedure, we do something quite different. When we meet new prospective enrollees we give them, nowadays, an ideological and philosophical presentation much more sophisticated than anything we used to do. So in fact, the way we implement it is much more filtering than anything we ever had before, because we go to a lot of pains to try to make them self-eliminate, to try to get them to examine carefully whether in fact their ideology is compatible with the school. I contend that if we were faced with a situation where our open enrollment was really ever tested, if we actually had a hundred people walking through the door without any interest in having an interview, without any interest in the trial week, just laying down the tuition—I mean, let's assume somebody just said, "Why, if a hundred of us get together and pay the money, we've got a majority of votes in the Assembly. We can go there for a year, get ourselves high school diplomas, and go out into the world." Imagine, a hundred people just suddenly get that realization and walk into the school and put down the tuition and take the school over. [5] They don't want to do anything violent or malicious to others, they don't want to take over the buildings, or anything like that; they just want diplomas, they want to turn the school into a diploma mill. So they

---

[5] The actual admissions/enrollment procedure has undergone many transformations since 1971.

hang around and, while here, they obey the law book in every detail. Such an occurrence would destroy the school. The only reason we are keeping our open enrollment policy is because we are monitoring it very carefully. The minute we would see a tremendous breach that showed that the ideological and philosophical filter wasn't functioning at all, we would probably have a whole new procedure instituted overnight. I'm sure of it. Because we couldn't tolerate it. We always have had a small but significant number of people who simply are peripheral to what the school is really about. It is true that they can have a change of heart at any time, and really become part of the school. But in fact the majority of these peripheral people don't; and the reason the school can survive with them in it is because there are not that many, they are not that overwhelming. We know very well that if the whole school was made up of the kind of people who are peripheral, it would fold. We wouldn't feel we were getting anywhere.

Take our stance toward the public. This has also had a dual nature all along. We have operated with the hope that we would have excellent relations with the community. I'm not talking about being polite, or "nice." I mean more than that. We really hoped that we would be able to make contact with people, and affect them as a result of this contact; that what we were doing wasn't that different, that they would see the light. When we go to a university and talk to a class in education, I have a sense sometimes that we're like people selling student participation or open classroom or the Leicestershire system—and we're treated that way often. Now, it isn't so surprising that we are treated that way, but we often respond that way too. It's as if the professor is parading all the new wares, and Sudbury Valley is one of the possibilities of the new model car that the class might buy. And we often fall right in with this. We describe our program—the way we run the day, the way our school is administered, what we do with the kids, and anecdotes, and so forth. That's a reformist point of view. Every now and then when we go to schools to speak, we get very aggressive. We simply walk into the room and say, "Look, we're not just another school with another curriculum; we've got a fundamentally different attitude toward people. For goodness sake, let's get that clear. What we're talking about is a central moral issue. Etc." It's the same with our relations to schools and organizations. We have had this hope that people interested in education, and people interested in reform and innovation, will be interested in us. Actually, as any revolutionary knows, nobody is more inimical to him than the reformer; because the reformer thinks that the system is basically all right, and that if people only accept his few changes, everything will be perfect. The worst thing on earth for a reformer is a revolutionary, who attacks the system at its core. By contrast, a person who is relatively conservative, stuck in the system, may suddenly wake up one morning and find out that he really hates it, and then join your revolution. But the reformer thinks *he's* got the answer, and it's not yours, and it's not a major transformation of everything. So basically the reformer is the real conservative, whereas the guy who is stuck in a rut is grist for the revolutionary mill. We've been wooing reformers, time and time again. We've been pleased to be called innovative, to be listed with alternative schools, etc. Whereas if we were adopting a revolutionary strategy, we would recognize that these are our most severe opponents and put them at arm's length.

Consider our approach toward staff hiring. When we introduced the concept of market value into staff hiring, we were talking about a reformist concept[6]. And there's another one: the no-tenure idea. We were looking at the school as one among many schools when we talked about market value. We are assuming that people can, or would want to, take jobs anywhere, elsewhere, maybe not even in a school. And when we talk about no tenure, we are talking about a purely business-like approach to education: if teachers are all right, they're all right; if they're not all right, we get rid of them, and they just have to find something else to do. The no-tenure policy, as we have formally treated it in our literature, doesn't take into account the importance to any revolutionary movement of committed people. Of course, in *carrying out* our no-tenure policy, we always rehired the committed people, so the formal policy didn't do us any harm. The way we have carried out the policy is to act as if the key to being hired is being committed, and one has to prove his commitment year in, year out. We might have said openly that hiring is a matter of commitment, but that is not the grounds on which we said the staff is hired. My point, again, is that these two trends are functioning in the school side by side. We didn't give the no-tenure policy the formal content that would have reflected its real value to the school. The formal content that we gave it was one that could be very familiar to other institutions. Other institutions have tenure, we have no tenure. We always said that if a teacher is successful, if he's useful

---

[6] The idea of tying compensation to market value was used for a short period of time in the early 1970's. It has not been used since.

to the school, if he fulfills the needs of the School Meeting at any given time—the kind of language that was perfectly familiar in any other milieu—he'd be hired, and that students deserve a hand in selecting their faculty. Whereas I maintain that side by side with the way we talked about it, and sounded very familiar to other reformist movements in other institutions, in fact we were implementing a different policy. We were using the no-tenure policy as a means of filtering out non-committed people. And we've never had the guts to come out and say that. To say that the real criterion according to which we hire staff is their commitment to the school, not their usefulness to the school. We've rehired people whom we have not even known how to justify, in ordinary terms, but the one thing we all have known is that they are committed. In fact, we've got a group of people year in, year out who are committed, and there isn't a dream of not rehiring them, the committed ones; it's just insanity not to. It's not because we need their educational skills. Or even all their services. Some services we do need—I'm not saying we don't need services; but the key reason we hire people is commitment. So, in effect, we don't really have a no tenure policy. In effect what we have is a constant annual purge—if you want to use a word that has fallen into disrepute; we clean ourselves. Regularly. Of the people who really aren't committed to the system that we are trying to promulgate.

The last thing I want to mention is our attitude toward visitors. Our whole visitors policy has been reformist in nature. We just let the people come in, because we hope. It's odd, because in this area it does us the most damage. If you're really close enough to the norms of the community at large so that you are simply correcting them, then a day's visit is enough. The reason our visitors are dissatisfied so many times is that they are looking at a place that has a different set of basic assumptions; they don't begin to understand it. They don't have the language. They don't have the bearings. So a reformist visitors' policy turns out to be catastrophic. Recently we have begun to say we would filter them out. We have them planning in advance. They write letters, so at least they are interested enough to write; we've been playing with the idea of charging admissions fees[7]. These are first glimmerings. Our earlier policy was a bother to the school, not because of the number of visitors who came. If twenty people a day who were committed to the idea of the school, or were really serious about it visited and roamed the school, nobody would have complained.

III

I would like to end by considering what our strategy should be in the future, once we've come to the point where we recognize clearly for the first time that, given the society around us and the culture that we are in, we are basically a revolutionary institution. Here we are with this realization. The question is, what do we do with it?

It seems to me we have three choices. One of them isn't really a choice. We could simply say, "Now that we suddenly really realize what we are, let's forget the whole thing and go off to the south seas. We have to fact that we're out of tune with everything. Goodbye." I don't think that's really a choice. I think that, being in our fourth year

---

[7] These fees were subsequently instituted.

of operation, we're well beyond that. We may be driven out some day, but I don't think we'll leave voluntarily.

The second choice is to purify our strategy; to realize what we are and to adopt an overall revolutionary strategy, and the tactics to match, so that we will have a coherent strategy right now. Not just to be pure, but to be more effective, if indeed it is more effective.

The third possibility is to continue the present mix of tactics.

We're aiming at success. We've got a revolutionary ideology, and we're aiming to succeed. But, as I said before, we also have to survive. So it becomes a question of goals. Our ultimate goal is to transform the culture so that it accepts and adopts the basic ideals we stand for. The question is, how do we get there? My conclusion is that every revolutionary movement in its early years has to adopt reformist trappings simply in order to survive. It has to be able to co-opt enough of the community's sympathy, cooperation, hangers-on that aren't committed, simply to keep it going, to keep it from being wiped out, until it has developed enough committed people to reach the takeoff point. The reason is simple: our society is not committed to pluralism sufficiently to allow groups with basically different world views to coexist and flourish. There is too much of a drive toward homogeneity, and too much violence. We have encountered this ourselves in countless areas. For example, enrollees and their families are subjected to enormous and incessant pressures by their friends, relations and neighbors for being involved in Sudbury Valley School. The "flak" is out of all proportion to the reality and would never be present if these people were simply going to an ordinary school (or even a reformist one). But the way things are today, the community simply does not have the tolerance to bear with equanimity the existence in its midst of people with a lifestyle that differs basically from the lifestyle of the majority. The same kind of violent opposition meets us on every front, everywhere, and turns our fight for survival into a never-ending struggle with opposing forces that never tire or give up. For this reason, we, and others in our position, *need* to develop and present a reformist side as an elemental tactic to keep alive.

What's important for us, though, is to realize what we're doing: to be self-conscious about it. Because, as I said earlier, by way of example, if we suddenly find that some of these reformist trappings were playing havoc with us, like the open enrollment suddenly letting in a whole slew of people that are very destructive, we have to know what we're really after and not let that happen. And I think that we have to be very careful in every area. For example, I think we really have to give serious thought, again, to visitors. That has been a very knotty problem. Is what we've done now going to be enough? We've got to keep a very close watch on it. Is our new procedure enough to keep to a manageable level disturbance that our reformist visitors policy creates? Or are we going to have to tighten it even more, and just filter out, as visitors, the committed or potentially people?

I think that eventually, when we do find more and more people who are committed to the whole lifestyle we represent, a lot of the minor problems that we have now are just not going to exist. For example, the staff-hiring, salary-tuition cycle is something that I see us breaking out of. It's bound to finally reach the point when we're a large, stable community of committed people. Just as today it's not in question that the staff is committed to keeping the school alive and promulgating its philosophy, so then it won't be in question that a much larger community will be committed to putting up enough money and enough resources to keep the whole enterprise afloat. There is going to be a natural commitment. The day will come when we'll have it, and we won't even have to discuss it. It will equilibrate itself. Everybody—parents, students, and staff—will realize that we have to do everything we can in order to keep the place going. It will be their way of life. They will have to support it. They will have no choice.

Today, we are just beginning. We have started with a large staff of committed people, and we added to that several families and outside individuals. Over the coming years, we're going to add more. That's the process that we are looking to.

There's a related point. In this matter of individual commitment, I have always felt that when a person decides *firmly* to make a radical departure, then he *can* make it. We say this often at the school. Generally no one will do this until he is desperate enough to take a large step; but then he will take it and there will be for him *no alternative* to taking it, no choice. All this holds for a single person. When it comes to establishing something like a school, or a community, or a movement, where other people are involved, *you* personally may be ready to make the commitment, but it's something that involves the cooperation of other people. So, until other people are around who will make the same commitment with you, no matter how desperate you are, you alone can't take the step. You've got to wait until others come around. That's why it's not enough just to float a revolution, to have an individual or two who have made an irrevocable commitment to it. That will suffice to get the motor sputtering, but it won't get the whole machine going. The enterprise as a whole will get going only when there are enough people doing the same thing, so that there will be a group large enough to make it a viable enterprise. That's what we have to hang on and wait for, always remembering that we have constantly got to monitor our tactics to maximize the number of committed people who join us.

This stance has come very immediate implications in detail. For example, let's take an aspect of the publicity policy, governing where you go to speak, and how. Now, say you were adopting a pure revolutionary strategy. In that case, you would go anywhere, anytime to relay your message, and the message would always be revolutionary. You would take any platform you could, and fees wouldn't be a consideration. Of course, if you get them, it's nice, but they are irrelevant to your goal: you would go for the purpose of delivering your message. Now, we have indeed gone everywhere, but once we went, we would as often as not deliver a reformist message. My point is that it would be retrogressive now to adopt a reformist policy—an establishmentarian one—and say that now we'd only go for big fees (which is something I once advocated, not long ago, and now realize to have been a mistake). That's super-reformist. "I'll only go for a fee, and I'll only go if you do this, and I'll only go if you do that"—we shouldn't do that at all. That's letting the reformist trappings take over. We should still go everywhere we can. And we should try to carry our revolutionary message everywhere we go. But every now and then, when our sense of judgement indicates that the audience's intolerance will not allow our message to be heard without causing us harm, we may adopt a reformist stance. That's what I would say is, in a very limited area, the lesson for today: go anywhere; forget about the fees; welcome any platform' and a priori go with the full gestalt of your revolutionary message to be said; but be prepared when you get there, and you get a sense of violence or hostility at the meeting, to tone it down to a reformist message. Similarly beware of situations where you know you are being used—for example, where you are being invited by a reformist group who are not really interested in Sudbury Valley, but who want to use the school as window dressing for their own schemes. There are times when, to further your exposure, you might allow yourself to be used, especially when you are so weak and need exposure so badly. On such occasions, you will have to deliver a reformist message, if only to avoid being blacklisted! Eventually, when you're much stronger, and you'll have more accessibility to platforms, you'll never even have to think of that. You'll always simply hammer away at your revolutionary message.

In the area of staff hiring policy, there is no reason to hide the criteria that we really use for hiring. I think we ought to admit that what really counts in a staff member is the degree of his commitment to what we are doing. We ought to acknowledge that this is the criterion according to which we are presently hiring. If this is recognized, it will be easier to settle things like disbursement policy, too, since people will realize why they are here. I see no virtue in the "this is a job like any other job" attitude. We may as well realize that we're here because we're committed, and we've got to make a go of it, and we'll just have to see to it that people are taken care of the best we can. It's similar in some respects to our earlier attitudes, but much more sophisticated, I think. The reason the early one fizzled out was precisely because we were saddled with elements of a reformist attitude. We underestimated the degree to which commitment and perseverance and revolutionary stance were important. And not simply commitment to person A or person B, nor even one only to the school, but as commitment *to the cadre*. To the school as the basis for a cadre, a cadre that has to be kept alive and enlarged. You can't afford to lose anybody. In the past, you could still be committed to the school as an education institution and lost one or two people—and say to yourself, "The school will go on." But the time has come to realize that you've got to be committed to the cadre, which means you can't afford to lose a single person if you can possibly keep him.

One more point. Our strategy must include definite provisions for cultivating people who we feel are likely to be additions to the cadre. It's this that I am afraid we haven't touched upon at all. I think that the time has come for us somehow to find a mechanism to tighten our bonds with those of the Assembly who are members either out of a present sense of commitment or a growing and nurturable sense of commitment. To do something definite with them, not just let them drift. The only place we presently cultivate the cadre is in the School Meeting. But for the wider group that could be terrifically useful, we have no means of cultivation; and this isn't limited to parents. A former student recently volunteered on her own that there was one thing she was continuing to do: "I'm constantly spreading the word and trying to get other people to be interested." Right now we have no mechanism for keeping that kind of contact alive; we're not even thinking in those directions. Whereas we should be able to identify people who are really committed to the idea of the school and who are ready to do something for it. The faster we do this, the faster we'll enlarge our cadre outside the staff. We've got to find a way to enable them to participate along with the rest of us.

I think that if our basic stance now is to be revolutionary, and to be aware that we are only using reformist trappings to the extent that we need them for survival, it will enable us to focus much more on the essentials, and to more rapidly discover the people who really want to come together through the school.